empowering communities

A Casebook from West Sudan

Peter Strachan with Christopher Peters

Oxfam UK and Ireland

Dedication

To the memory of those staff and partners of Oxfam Darfur who have lost their lives during the implementation of the Kebkabiya Project:
  Shertai Adam Ahmedai
  Abdel Moneim Abakora Ahmeda
  Ebada Abdel Gabbar
  Adam Ibrahim

Nesal Allah Lihum Ar Rahma Wa Il Maghfira

نسأل الله لهم الرحمة والمغفرة

facing page fetching water near Bora village, Sudan

Published by Oxfam UK and Ireland
First published 1997

© Oxfam UK and Ireland 1997

A catalogue record for this publication is available from the British Library.

ISBN 0 85598 358 2

All rights reserved. Reproduction, copy, transmission, or translation of any part of this publication may be made only under the following conditions:

- with the prior written permission of the publisher; or
- with a licence from the Copyright Licensing Agency Ltd., 90 Tottenham Court Road, London W1P 9HE, UK; or
- for quotation in a review of the work; or
- under the terms set out below.

This publication is copyright, but may be reproduced by any method without fee for teaching purposes, but not for resale. Formal permission is required for all such uses, but normally will be granted immediately. For copying in any other circumstances, or for re-use in other publications, or for translation or adaptation, prior written permission must be obtained from the publisher, and a fee may be payable.

Published by Oxfam UK and Ireland, 274 Banbury Road, Oxford OX2 7DZ, UK
(registered as a charity, no. 202918)

Available in Ireland from Oxfam in Ireland, 19 Clanwilliam Terrace, Dublin 2 (tel. 01 661 8544). Addresses of agents and distributors are given on the last page.

Designed by Oxfam Design Department OX414/RB/97
Printed by Oxfam Print Unit

Oxfam UK and Ireland is a member of Oxfam International.

Front cover photo: Suzanne Jaspers/Oxfam

Contents

Acknowledgements v

Preface vii

Introduction 1

- 1 Background to the project 5
- 2 Service provision: the technical perspective 19
- 3 Involving the community 35
- 4 Participation and gender 47
- 5 Moving towards independence 61
- 6 Towards the future 77

References 87

Glossary of abbreviations 87

Empowering communities

above Farrah Omer Bello, Oxfam project coordinator (left),
and Omer Idris, Chair, Kebkabiya Smallholders Charitable Commitee (right).

Acknowledgements

My first debt of gratitude must be to the Oxfam team on the Kebkabiya project who remembered me sufficiently kindly from my days as the organisation's Darfur Representative during the years 1987-90 to invite me back to Darfur to write a report on the project. The resultant fieldwork for this book was undertaken in November 1994. I would especially like to thank Farrah Omer Bello, now Kebkabiya Project Co-ordinator, who organised such an effective programme for me in Kebkabiya, Hussein Abdallah, former Kebkabiya project officer now working in the Darfur Regional office in El Fasher, who did an exemplary job as my field assistant during the research for this report and Musa Mohammed Sanan, our driver, who completed the field team which made my time in Darfur working on this report such an enjoyable experience. I am also extremely grateful to Omer Idris, Chair of the Kebkabiya Smallholders' Charitable Society, and all his colleagues in the Society who gave me a fantastic welcome and large quantities of their time to enable me to come to as full an understanding as possible of their achievements and aspirations.

I must also thank Oxfam's staff in both Khartoum and El Fasher for making the arrangements that enabled this visit to go so smoothly. Especial thanks are due to Salih Abdel Mageed, Kebkabiya Project Co-ordinator from 1988 to 1994 and now Regional Programme Manager in El Fasher, and to John Buttery, Liz Gascoigne, Sheilagh Holmes, Anita Heaver, and Christian Gudgeon, who all played their part in putting the project together and getting me properly briefed and on my way. Catherine Robinson and Sarah Totterdell were invaluable in helping to get the book into its final form.

Most of all, though, I must thank my wife, Claire, for her solid support of my prolonged absence in Darfur and numerous less prolonged ones on the computer and among piles of Kebkabiya reports, at a most difficult time in our lives.

Peter Strachan

Empowering communities

below children tending livestock, Sahel

Preface

This book describes the Kebkabiya project in North Darfur, Sudan, from its inception as an 'operational' project run by Oxfam, to the setting up of the Kebkabiya Smallholders' Charitable Society (KSCS) and eventual handover of responsibility for the project activities to the KSCS as an Oxfam partner.

The original text was an account of the project written by Peter Strachan at the request of Oxfam's staff in Kebkabiya and the Management Committee of the KSCS, because they felt that the story of their success, and the hard road to achieving that success, would be of interest to many people interested in development. 'Success' is a word too often missing from books on relief and development, but the Kebkabiya project merits the term: it is an example of successful rural community development based upon participatory democracy, and community project management and accountability. Peter Strachan's account of the Kebkabiya project is both exciting and informative. Exciting in that it attempts to convey the experience of people actually involved in a development project; informative in that it provides numerous examples of how concepts such as empowerment, community participation, and gender equity—concepts which are fundamental to Oxfam's approach—are put into practice within a particular cultural, social, and economic context; and also because it offers a unique insight into the process of handing over an operational project to a local partner.

It was because of this feeling of excitement and the belief that valuable lessons could be learnt from the project that Oxfam decided to use the account of the Kebkabiya project as the basis of the first in a series of Development Casebooks, which were conceived as detailed studies of particular projects or programmes which provide examples of innovative practice transferable to other contexts. Chris Peters was asked to edit the draft for publication, to draw out the particular points of interest. *Empowering Communities* is about the evolution of a directly-managed, operational response by an international aid agency to a major emergency, into a community-managed rural development project, carrying out a range of activities. It shows how the participation in the project management on the part of men and women from local communities was encouraged from an early stage, and how that participation became a means of empowering communities; and considers issues arising from the transfer of power and responsibility from an aid agency to a partner organisation. The problems and difficulties of such an evolution which had to be resolved are not, of course, specific to Kebkabiya or the KSCS; it is this fact that gives the Kebkabiya experience such importance in the broader context of the work of Oxfam and other NGOs.

Throughout the text, liberal use has been made of the words of those involved in the project, in order to give a more immediate and personal dimension to the account. Inevitably, the quotations as they appear in the text are reconstructions of what was actually said. Quite apart from the necessity of making them self-explanatory to the reader with no knowledge of the immediate project area or issues, the words have been translated from the Arabic and, in the case of women's words, often from Fur into Arabic and then into English. The 'quote' has, finally, had to be reconstituted from notes hastily taken in the field, sometimes after an interval of a few days.

The structure of the book is as follows: after an introductory section, giving a brief account of the history of the project, the first chapter gives some background information, on the area, the social relationships within the communities with which Oxfam worked, and Oxfam's approach to development. The second chapter describes the various technical interventions undertaken in the course of the project in detail, with some indication of how the community was involved. This involvement is dealt with more fully in chapter three, where the various structures which enabled participation of local people are outlined. One of the major problems which Oxfam faced was how to ensure that women were consulted and involved in the management of the project, and benefited from the various activities. The issue of women's participation is covered in chapter four. The next chapter describes the process of operational, management, and financial handover of the project from Oxfam to the community. The final chapter draws out the lessons which the project offers, and looks ahead to consider options for the future.

Introduction

After the excellent rains of 1994, the village of Somati in Northern Darfur was a beautiful place to visit: tucked away under the Jebel Si mountains. it was surrounded by rolling green pastures, flourishing acacia trees, and fields of healthy millet awaiting harvest.

Back in 1984, however, Somati presented a very different picture. The rains had failed for three years in succession and the people were in a desperate state. Halima Idris vividly recalls that year:

> ❜ It was a very difficult time, a horrible period. We could only eat one meal a day and sometimes not even that. We would just sit there all day feeling hungry. In the early days after the grain ran out we would make a porridge from water-melon seeds. Then the water-melon seeds ran out and we would go out to collect *mukheit* berries: they are bitter and it takes days to soak the poison out of them, but at least they are something to eat. It was all we had and if we didn't find any then we couldn't eat.

> I would go down to Kebkabiya to ask for work on the building sites. If I found any work I would work for a few days at a time, until I had enough money to buy some food, and then I would take it back to the village for my children. I had three children at that time, aged ten, eight, and two. They fell sick from hunger though mercifully all of them survived. Many other children in the village actually died. My animals were not so lucky. I lost about 30 of my goats during the famine — most of my flock. ❜

above Halima Idris recalls the drought of 1984

Empowering communities

For the European overseas aid charities the crisis in western Sudan posed a peculiar problem. The government of Jafaar Nimeiri, then in power, had attempted to conceal the true situation, and food shortages had become full-blown famine when reports finally reached the outside world. Publicised with enormous success by the fundraising efforts of Bob Geldof, the plight of the people of Sudan and Ethiopia touched the conscience of Europe, and funds for relief work were more freely available to organisations such as Oxfam than ever before. However, given the time necessary to obtain relief supplies and then transport them across more than a thousand miles of harsh and roadless terrain, it was a virtual impossibility to spend all of the money on food to put into the mouths of the hungry. Although the funds had been raised for the immediate relief of starvation, what was really needed at this stage was assistance with getting people's lives back to normal after the famine. Relief food that arrived too late would merely flood the post-famine market, and depress the price of food produced by local farmers after the good rains of 1985. People needed long-term help to become less vulnerable to future periods of drought and crop failure.

Halima Idris takes up the story again:

> The period of relief lasted for about four or five months. We were able to survive on the grain brought to us by the Save the Children Fund, and our sick children could be treated in the clinics that they set up. Then we had to prepare for the rainy season, but the problem was that, before the relief arrived, in order to survive we had eaten the seeds that we had put away. And we were so weakened by hunger that we didn't have the strength to plant.
>
> Our village sheikh had been to meetings in Segering, the major village in this area, where he had met with Oxfam to discuss the establishment of a seedbank there that would serve this village and the others in the area. The idea that they had agreed upon was that Oxfam would distribute seeds to us for planting, but we would have to pay them back — and some extra — when we brought in our harvest. The hope was that we would then build up a reserve that we could draw upon in future times of hardship. I borrowed ten bowls of millet seeds from the seedbank and divided them into two. We used half of them for food to give us the strength to work, and planted some of the rest. The first planting was destroyed by rats and grasshoppers as soon as it had germinated, but eventually we did get a crop.
>
> Since then I have borrowed seeds from the seedbank every year. Oxfam has worked with the committee that was established to manage

the seedbank to develop the project so that it provides lots of other services now. For instance, there is a veterinary worker in Segering, trained by Oxfam and using drugs provided through Oxfam, who covers this village too. When my goats were sick last year I was able to take them to him for injections to cure them.

This project has greatly improved the conditions in the village. In the past, if we wanted to get seed or to have our animals treated or receive any other agricultural services we had to go to Kebkabiya, which is three hours away by donkey or more on foot, and purchase them at black-market prices. Realistically speaking that usually meant that they were not available to people in this village. But since the project began we have been able to meet regularly with Oxfam staff and discuss our actual needs with them. This means that everyone has a say. Before, if I wanted to give my views to the authorities I would have to leave my children here and go to Kebkabiya to try to find the appropriate official.

I like to think that we will never have a return to the conditions of 1984, but I think that if we did face another period of hunger we would more easily be able to endure it because we would go into it in a stronger position. *

At its inception, the Kebkabiya project was simply an attempt to increase food security as a long-term response to a major famine. The initial objective was to establish 12 seedbanks, and it was during this first phase that Oxfam staff gained a clearer sense of other perceived problems in the communities in the area. The second phase of the project, which began in 1989, introduced several new interventions in an attempt to address these identified problems, with components in animal health, animal traction, pest control, soil and water conservation, and community development. Though coordinated by a professional Oxfam staff team, this phase was implemented in conjunction with a democratic structure of community representation, and the eventual necessity of some kind of handover began to be considered. Whereas the seedbanks had been managed by local committees, which followed a traditional pattern, being almost exclusively male, and nominated by existing authorities within the villages, the new Village Centre Committees, which were created to oversee the activities undertaken in the second phase of the project, were far more democratic. Each village from a group of five to twelve villages elected one man and one woman to represent it on a committee which met in a central village. In turn, each Village Centre Committee elected one man and one woman to a Project Management Committee, which met in Kebkabiya town. In late 1990, the PMC decided to register as an independent body, and the Kebkabiya Smallholders' Charitable Society came into being as a legal entity. There was now an organisation to which responsibility for the project could eventually be handed over by Oxfam.

Oxfam usually operates by funding existing organisations with which it can form a partnership to take forward development activities. But when Oxfam began to work in Kebkabiya, not only were there considerable funds to be spent, which had been donated by the UK public in response to the emergency in the region, but there were no suitable local groups who could carry out development projects in the way Oxfam and its donors would find acceptable. This was the reason why Oxfam itself set up a diverse development programme, and became 'operational', taking full responsibility for employing and managing technical and support staff, and purchasing and distributing all inputs. When the time came to hand over this complex operational programme to the community it was set up to benefit, there were no models to follow, and many questions to be answered. What were the stages of a successful handover? What was likely to be the time-frame required? What would need to be accomplished during this period for handover to be successful and sustainable? How could Oxfam relinquish control without sacrificing the social gains for which it had struggled, especially in the field of gender equity? How could the participation in project management, on the part of women and men, be encouraged? Would the idea of democratic representation be fully accepted by the community? By what yardsticks may a successful handover be measured? Would there be a continuing role for Oxfam after handover had been effected?

Some answers to these questions, an account of how and why the project evolved as it did, and the many lessons to be learnt from the difficulties people faced, and the strategies they adopted to deal with them, will be found in the chapters that follow.

Background to the project   I

Before giving an account of the Kebkabiya project, it is first necessary to make clear the physical and social context in which Oxfam became operational, and some of the broad principles underlying the work of relief and development NGOs; and to give some background information to make clear why the particular development activities which the project encompassed were chosen.

Sudan

The Republic of Sudan covers an area of 996,757 square miles (2,503,890 square kilometres), approximately ten times the size of the UK. In terms of geography and climate, the country can be roughly divided into three broad bands: arid deserts in the north, savannah grasslands in the central region, and woodlands and swamp in the south, where annual rainfall can exceed 57 inches (1,465 millimetres).

The north-east corner of Sudan borders the Red Sea, with Port Sudan being the country's principal commercial port. To the north is Egypt; to the west, Chad and the Central African Republic; to the south, Zaïre, Uganda and Kenya, and, to the east, Eritrea and Ethiopia. Sudan's borders were largely demarcated under a Turco-Egyptian administration which ruled Sudan from 1820 until 1881, when there was a nationalist uprising led by the Mahdi (Mohammed Ahmed al Mahdi). The British intervened and deposed the Mahdi in 1898, and Sudan was placed under Anglo-Egyptian rule — the Condominium — until it achieved independence in 1956.

A diverse land; a diverse people

Sudan's current population of some 26.7 million people is made up of 19 major ethnic groups that can be further divided into 597 smaller sub-groupings, speaking over 100 different languages and several hundred different dialects. The majority of Sudanese, some 57 per cent, are pastoralists and subsistence farmers, living in a harsh environment. The average population density of Sudan is just ten persons per square kilometre, but there are marked regional variations. Approximately two million people still follow a nomadic or semi-nomadic lifestyle.

Empowering communities

above map of Sudan

A history of uneven development

Under the Condominium, economic development was concentrated largely in the central and eastern regions of the country. The first large-scale irrigated farming schemes were started in the central region of El Gezira in the 1920s to produce cheap cotton for the mills of Lancashire. Situated between the two great rivers, the Blue Nile and the White Nile, the Gezira remains the largest irrigated agricultural scheme in the world covering some 800,000 hectares of land. In 1944, mechanised farming began on the fertile lands of eastern Sudan.

After independence, economic development continued to focus on the Gezira, and on Kassala and Khartoum provinces, to the economic and social detriment of other areas of the country. Such economic policies, many of them promoted and financed by aid and development assistance from Western governments, were a primary cause of the civil war which began in 1956 and — apart from a period of peace from 1972-1983 — has continued to engulf parts of southern Sudan to the present day.

The south of the country has been the scene of major conflict between Government and anti-Government forces. Even those regions which lie outside the main areas of conflict have suffered from the effects of war. The economy has declined, and the incidence of inter-ethnic hostilities has increased.

However, in some regions, it was prolonged periods of drought, rather than the war as such, that caused the prolonged crises of the mid-1980s, and the widespread famine. One of these regions was Darfur.

Darfur

Until 1916, when the region was incorporated into the Anglo-Egyptian Condominium of Sudan, Darfur was an independent sultanate. This region is the westernmost part of present day Sudan. Darfur, which means the homeland of the Fur people, is not inhabited exclusively by the Fur, but is home to a number of different ethnic groups.

Darfur (recently subdivided into three States: Northern, Southern and Western Darfur) covers an area approximately the size of France and Spain put together. There are only three towns of any size: El Fasher, Nyala, and El Geneina. Much of the area is uninhabitable desert. Immediately south of the desert is the Sahel, a strip of marginal, semi-arid land, several hundred kilometres wide, which stretches all the way across Africa from the Red Sea coastline in Eritrea and Sudan, through Chad, Niger, Burkina Faso, Mali, and finally into Mauritania and Senegal, where it meets the Atlantic.

The Sahel is characterised by low rainfall and very fragile soils, mostly of sand that has blown off the desert over the previous thousand years or so and

Empowering communities

been stabilised by drought-resistant plants. Many of the people living in the Sahel are largely, if not exclusively, dependent upon livestock which roam across huge areas, grazing on the scanty pastures. For many of these people, especially in the northern reaches of the Sahel, nomadism is their whole way of life, as they follow the rains through the annual cycle with their herds to wherever the pasture is freshest and sweetest.

Further south, some agriculture becomes possible, using techniques evolved over the centuries to coax a harvest of a few especially hardy crops from the land. In these areas, people may either have adopted a 'semi- pastoralist' lifestyle, living in villages with some of the men departing with the herds for long periods of the year, or they may have become settled agriculturalists, rarely taking their animals more than a day's walk from their village.

Relations between different groups of nomads and between nomads and settled farmers have, for centuries, been based on a mixture of tolerance and need, expressed in shared access to water-points, recognised grazing rights, and reciprocal trade. However, relations have, from time to time, broken down, mainly during extended periods of drought when skirmishes between nomadic groups over diminishing resources of water and grazing land, or raids on agricultural lands, can occur. These outbreaks of hostility should perhaps be seen as part of a long-term survival strategy adopted to meet the demands of particular circumstances. In periods of good rains, different groups have lived in relatively peaceful equilibrium with each other.

However, during periods of drought in the mid-1980s and early 1990s, hostilities have increased in scale, intensified by increasing desertification and the disruptive effects of the long-running civil war on the economy and social structures.

below The mountainous regions around Kebkabiya

Kebkabiya

The monotony of the Sahel's flat expanses is broken up in Darfur by a number of volcanic mountain ranges. The highest of these is the dormant crater of the Jebel Marra and its foothills. The crater rises above the plain to some 3088 metres (10,000 feet approximately), and around its higher reaches hot springs still flow.

Below the northern foothills of the Jebel Marra is the administrative centre of Kebkabiya, a town of about 15,000 inhabitants. Kebkabiya town lies on the edge of a plain that extends as far as the smaller mountain range of the Jebel Si, some thirty miles to the north, and serves as the main market town and centre for the villages of the plain, the northern foothills of the Jebel Marra and the southern foothills of the Jebel Si. The rains here are usually better than in most other places of comparable latitude in Darfur because of the 'rain-shadow' effect produced by the proximity of the Jebel Marra.

Even this benign anomaly in the climate does not, however, always mean that good rains will occur, and the terrible drought conditions experienced during 1984 and 1985 were by no means unique in the recent history of the Kebkabiya area. Droughts and food shortages have occurred in 1888–92, 1913–4, 1926–7, 1930, 1939, 1941–2, 1969 and 1973 (de Waal, 1989).

Oxfam in Kebkabiya

It was primarily to reduce this ever-present threat of hunger that Oxfam turned its efforts from relief to development in the aftermath of the 1984-5 famine. What is the Oxfam approach to development? This is in a sense an unanswerable question, because the approach varies according to the context, but there are always common elements, one of which would be the involvement of the beneficiary community in project decision-making and implementation. Both 'involvement' and 'community' are complex and multi-faceted concepts. A funding organisation, however much it may be committed to the ideal of participation, inevitably has a great deal of power and control. While it may accept the obligation to listen to representatives of the community, the degree of involvement in decisions about development directions which the community may have in reality, is open to question. Similarly, while the community may be a fairly easily defined unit in the case of a small and precisely focused project such as the construction of a well in a single village, for a project like that in Kebkabiya, targeted at up to 66,000 people in 120 villages scattered across a large geographical area, it is much harder to define. What were the existing social structures within these villages, with which Oxfam might work?

Structures of authority and service delivery

Village authorities

The villages within the Kebkabiya area have an acknowledged head, usually the sheikh of the village. Although the sheikh will be responsible for resolving most of the problems and disputes that arise, this will often be in consultation with other men in the village. In major issues affecting the whole village the sheikh will have considerable influence but will only be able to carry the day if he can persuade the majority of the other men to accept his ideas.

There are other acknowledged authorities within the village. Matters relating to personal morality and religion will fall within the sphere of the Imam; the distribution of sugar allocations from the governmental authorities and decisions about requests for special purposes such as a wedding are the responsibility of a separate committee formed specially for that purpose. In addition, each tribe has its own social organisation on a wider level. In the case of the Fur tribe, by far the largest in the Kebkabiya project area, the paramount authority is the Shertai of the Fur, who lives in Kebkabiya town.

Local government structures and service provision

Within the formal structures of government, the village will send representatives to a Village Council that might cover half a dozen or more settlements. These Councils report to a Rural Council, one of several that make up an Area Council. Until recently there were three Rural Councils in Kebkabiya Area Council, and the project worked in only the largest of these: the Kebkabiya Rural Council. (At the time of writing, Kebkabiya Rural Council is being divided into two with the eastern half becoming the Jebel Si Rural Council.) The government civil servants who serve these Councils work closely with Council members at all levels. This is particularly so since the recent reforms of the Councils into Popular Committees (*Lijan Shaabiya*).

In practice, membership of the traditional and formal authority structures are likely to overlap, thus ensuring that governmental policy is implemented with the added authority of the traditional leadership. Noor El Din, Head of the Popular Committee for Kebkabiya Area, explains:

> ❝ Although previous governments in Sudan have sought to further rural development, they have failed because, like the governments of most developing countries, they lacked resources. The approach of the current regime is to emphasise grassroots participation.
>
> Rather than telling communities what will be the centrally planned initiatives to be undertaken in their area, we seek to empower them by making available to them through the Popular Committees the resources that they require and allowing them to chose their own priorities.

Background to the project

The relationship with the traditional leaders is very close and their authority is wholly recognised by the Popular Committees. The tasks of ensuring security in their area and of environmental conservation are wholly delegated to them. These tasks are under the supervision of the formal authority structures so that extra resources can be made available when necessary. It's also very common to find that the traditional leaders sit on the Popular Committees for their areas, so long as they are chosen to do so by the people themselves. ❜

Service delivery and international development agencies

Another vehicle of service delivery of which the Kebkabiya communities had experience prior to Oxfam involvement in the area were the international agencies who were operational during the period of famine relief. Although nominally committed to a participatory way of working, aid agencies, including Oxfam, when involved in large-scale emergency relief operations, may not always be able to live up to their own rhetoric. While participation and emergency relief are not mutually exclusive, they are nevertheless notoriously difficult to combine, particularly in large operations such as those mounted during the famine period. It was therefore hardly surprising that the relief programmes were seen by the villagers as free, if highly appreciated, hand-outs. Such welfare-orientated programmes, planned by technical experts within the agencies and the Regional Government, remained outside the control of the villagers.

Working with communities

While Oxfam has always sought to work harmoniously with both the traditional and formal authorities, its belief that the beneficiary community should always be involved in development activities meant that from the beginning it encouraged the creation of a different structure through which that community would be consulted and represented.

There were two main reasons for this, one theoretical and the other very practical. The theoretical reason was to do with Oxfam's view of the nature of poverty: that poverty is to be measured not only in terms of resources but also in terms of power and marginalisation from it. The more remote people are from the sources of power, be it political or economic, then the poorer they are likely to be. People who understand and can influence the systems that control resources in any community will use that influence to ensure that they share as fully as possible in whatever resources are available. It follows that an organisation committed to working with the poorest, such as Oxfam, will have to look critically at the existing systems of representation, and may need to move beyond them.

The practical fact follows from the above theoretical point. Within the community at Kebkabiya, women are demonstrably poorer than men, and they are also almost totally excluded from existing decision-making structures. As the project's experience was to demonstrate, their poverty is at least in part due to the fact that men's arrogation of power has excluded women almost completely from the distribution of resources within the communities. Female-headed households are systematically poorer than male-headed ones; married women are poorer than their husbands. If the whole community — men and women — were to be involved in and benefit from development, Oxfam would have to work with the community to create a new system of representation, and a new kind of committee structure.

Because this structure would exercise control over material resources and give access to organisational strength and contacts with political decision-makers, it came to be a new source of power within the community. In the ten years during which the project has been operational in Kebkabiya, Oxfam has, in the words of the Fur Shertai in Kebkabiya, become 'a member and an integral part of the community'. How has a foreign development organisation evolved such a local perception of itself?

A fresh approach to service delivery

We need to return to the question of what is meant by the 'involvement' of the community. For Oxfam, any intervention that is effectively to tackle poverty necessarily entails the transfer of control over resources, be they material or technical, to poor people. To the communities of Kebkabiya this was a new concept in terms of service delivery. For operational government Ministries, with historical links to the colonial period, extensive consultation and the active encouragement of participation by the community in development programmes was also an alien concept. Even for civil servants genuinely committed to a more community-based model of development, and there are many who are, such an approach would have been difficult, given the resource starvation of the Ministries. Consultation is highly time-consuming, requires budgets for transport and field allowances for staff, and raises expectations in a way that would not be justifiable if the resources were not then available to meet them. It would, furthermore, be likely to be treated with suspicion by villagers used to the political manipulation of governmental machinery.

Communities in Kebkabiya

'Community' is another term which can have widely different interpretations. In order to work effectively in Kebkabiya, Oxfam first needed to gain a deeper understanding of the local communities: the ways in which social interactions took place, how power was exercised, the extent and nature of poverty, and how people prioritised the need for change. Therefore over a period of two months in 1985, the first of several socio-economic surveys was conducted in order to gain this understanding and then evaluate a number of possible development interventions. The process of gathering such information also established, from the beginning, a dialogue with different groups and individuals which, over time, instilled a sense of trust between local people and Oxfam. People began to believe that Oxfam valued local inputs into a project that was to be built upon the long-term involvement of the agency. Thus local knowledge and skills, perceptions of vulnerability, needs and rights, and possible solutions to enhancing food security and livelihoods, were utilised in project planning. In this way, the local people involved were encouraged to see themselves as stakeholders in a development process, not the passive recipients of other people's solutions to their problems. However, as we shall see, there were occasions when people were not fully consulted, with unfortunate consequences.

Defining the target groups: who are the poorest of the poor, and why

Following the socio-economic studies, Oxfam initially investigated the feasibility of enhancing food production on small plots of land in villages with access to the rich alluvial soils along the seasonal watercourses known as *wadis* that carry the annual rains down off the mountain and eventually south to the swamps of the Central African Republic. Farms on *wadi* land can use irrigation round the year to grow a variety of profitable crops such as citrus fruits, tomatoes, and vegetables. It very rapidly became clear that the major differences in the Kebkabiya area were less those between rich and poor within villages than those between rich and poor villages — the defining criterion being that of whether or not the village had access to *wadi* land.

Villages without *wadi* land are wholly dependent upon the crops they can grow from the fragile sandy soils that typify the Sahel, known in Arabic as *goz*, and of course upon their goats and other animals. *Goz* cannot realistically be irrigated. If the rains are good then farmers can expect a reasonable yield of the local staple — millet — some ground-nuts for sale as a cash crop, and saleable quantities of the other crops that are grown on *goz* in Darfur, such as watermelon, chilli, black-eyed beans (*loubia*), hibiscus (*kirkade*) and sesame. *Goz* farmers are almost entirely at the mercy of the annual rainfall for their livelihood. Therefore, with the exception of the abortive experiment described later, the focus of Oxfam's activities in Kebkabiya was henceforth to be emphatically upon the *goz* or rainfed sector.

Defining the 'household' in Kebkabiya

Before co-ordinating any project intervention, it is always essential for a development agency to investigate the basic collective units making up a community: the family and the household.[1] A family is defined through kinship, marriage and parenthood; a household as a residential unit where people are not necessarily all related; both can greatly vary in size and composition from culture to culture. For example, members of one family can live in different households, or marriages can take place within or outside the kin group.

In Kebkabiya, definition of a 'household' was problematic because the composition of a family unit was so variable and fluid. This situation was due partly to high rates of polygamy and seasonal and long-term male migration out of the area to find work. Being 'married' did not necessarily imply either the permanent co-residence of wife and husband, or that economic support and co-operation were provided within the family or household.

High rates of polygamy and a large household were, to some extent, linked to ownership of *wadi* land; while low rates of polygamy and smaller than average households tended to be found in villages that had only *goz* land. The management of these different types of land also had an effect on the individual household, and the division of labour within it, and whether marriages took place inside or outside the kin group.

Further, marriage in Darfur is not necessarily a single rite of passage, a movement from being 'unmarried' to being 'married', but rather a set of stages. After the wedding contract, the wife may continue to live with her parents until the dowry is fully paid, or even after this has occurred. The husband, during this period, will pay extended visits to his family-in-law's compound, until, after the dowry is paid, the couple may move into their own compound.

In all, four different household units were identified in the Kebkabiya project area, the product of a complex dynamic affecting and being affected by levels of resources, types of livelihood, kin relationships, and marriage practices.

---

1 Much of the material in the remaining sections of this chapter is based on the extensive research and evaluations carried out by Brendan Gormley, Adrienne Martin, Nick Meadows, and Ann Muir, listed in the references.

Migration and the household

An analysis of the age structure of over 5,000 people resident in various parts of the project area, showed that 63 per cent of the recorded population were under 20 years of age and 40.3 per cent ten years old or under. In the 21 to 40 age group — 22.8 per cent of the recorded population — there are almost twice as many women as men.

The principle reason for this imbalance in sex ratios lies in out-migration by men to find work. Such out-migration is particularly prevalent in villages that have very limited access to alluvial — *wadi* — land, both in terms of the size of the plots, and its distribution. In such villages, married men formed a significant percentage of out-migrants.

In a sample of 22 villages, with a total population of 5,432, there were 909 married women, 631 married men present, and 112 married men absent. Of the women, 301 were widowed or divorced. Divorced men and men who had taken their families with them would increase the number of out-migrants, but exact figures were not researched. Added to this, many young boys were absent at Koranic schools, and many in the 16 to 20 age group were working in the main towns of Darfur. The period away from the household can vary from a few months to a year, but, in some cases, absences can be for several years, or lead to the migrant settling permanently away from his home village, and can also result in divorce.

Economic and social effects of migration

The level of cash remittances from male migrants back to the household appeared to be extremely low, although when migrants eventually return, they may bring cash with them. Most of the wages earned through migrant labour are not spent or invested in the rural household but in urban Darfur and central Sudan. Such lack of investment puts further pressure on local resources in traditional agricultural communities.

The work of maintaining the household — the rearing of children, feeding and clothing them and caring for the elderly and the sick — was carried out exclusively by women, and within female-headed households, as was the provision of shelter, and the fulfilment of social obligations. Women and men owned their own plots of land within the same household, and women provided up to 90 per cent of the labour power for subsistence agriculture. Women also determined the use of their land, particularly in the cultivation of *goz* soils. There was seldom any surplus produce available for sale. A small amount of cash for the household was provided from such activities as petty trading in tea, milk, and ghee in local markets, and the sale of firewood, and animal fodder. Women had little control over the use of any cash available;

their husbands and other male members of the family dictated how it was to be spent.

Women also migrate within Darfur on a seasonal basis, working on harvesting the crops or other agricultural work. This migration has increased as a result of drought and environmental decline. One consequence has been the increasing destitution of old people. With sons absent and daughters supporting their own children, many old people have no one to support them, and they go to Kebkabiya town, ekeing out a livelihood by begging.

The Oxfam study revealed that the smallholder farmers, working rain-fed land, were the poorest of all the social and economic groups in the project area. They had few other resources available to them, and were the most vulnerable to the effects of long-term environmental and economic decline. Because male out-migration was most prevalent amongst such smallholders, the numbers of women-headed households were significantly higher than in other groups.

Although a number of possible interventions that addressed the various needs of each group were possible, the establishment of seedbanks as a sustainable resource to help *goz* farmers was seen as the highest priority for an initial post-famine intervention.

Addressing gender inequalities

Although many discriminatory factors, such as property ownership, age, ethnicity, education, status, rights to particular resources or livelihoods, all influence the social impact and effectiveness of any development project on individuals and communities, a major social factor which underlies many other forms of discrimination is gender.

Oxfam's research confirmed that in Sudan, as in most other countries, men have more power in both the public and private spheres of their society than women; as a result, women are conditioned to perceive themselves as justly occupying a subordinate role within their society and to accept that men should exercise the greatest control over resources — resources which include women's own time and labour. Gender roles and relations, although often viewed as fixed and unchangeable, in fact, can change over time, and in response to changing circumstances. However, a change in gender relations can only occur from within a society, and cannot be imposed from without.

In chapter four, the particular position of women in relation to the project will be examined in detail. But here we must stress that gender analysis is not concerned only with women, but with the relationships between men and women. Women are often seen as a homogenous group; however, just as men have different vested interests and degrees of power and status, so do women.

Although gender relations are characterised by the inferior position of women within their social group, many men are also marginalised in relation to the wider society through different but parallel social processes. A gender-sensitive approach to development, although it may consist of specific interventions aimed exclusively at women, tries to base such interventions on an understanding of the ways in which people relate to one other within a wider framework.

However, there are always considerable difficulties for a development agency wishing to address gender inequalities. Perceptions of such inequalities are complex and differ in particular situations, with respect to particular activities, and among different groups of people. The degree to which women themselves question their position within their own society can vary enormously. Many women, particularly those who are most marginalised, often remain silent, or feel that a development programme is not intended for them. Other women may express their interests in terms of the welfare of their children or their household in general rather than of what they themselves might need or aspire to.

Why Oxfam became operational in Kebkabiya

As has been noted earlier, Oxfam's usual way of working in a country has been to identify local partner agencies with which it could work, providing funding and technical expertise and, in turn, learning about local solutions to local problems. Such a two-way process would then be synthesised into the broader Oxfam experience and passed on to other partners in the same region or in other countries. Typically such partner agencies would be a small local NGO or a community self-help group working in a fairly small-scale manner very close to the grassroots.

In Kebkabiya there were no local agencies with the management experience or the infrastructural strength to handle the type of work that both the community and Oxfam wished to realise; so the Kebkabiya project was 'operational'. That is, staff were employed to carry out the programmes under Oxfam's direct management. This departure from the standard participatory approach was more apparent than real. From the outset, the long-term aim was to maximise community involvement. The seedbanks were managed by local committees, who gradually took an increasing responsibility for management decisions. When the project moved into its second phase, a new system of representative committees was set up. The creation of the KSCS represented a further step towards community management and eventual handover.

Participation and social change

Societies are not fixed entities, but dynamic and complex systems of relationships that change and can be changed in a fluid, open-ended process. As we have seen, the reason for adopting a participatory approach to development is the belief that the root cause of poverty is the social and economic marginalisation experienced by people who have little or no control over the conditions in which they live. If Oxfam's intervention in Kebkabiya directed towards technical and social change were to be brought about largely through community-based structures, this would obviously lead to some degree of change within existing social relationships.

Such an approach has to address many complex problems. How, for example, are existing structures affected by — or resistant to — social and economic change? How do those structures affect the project's goals of maximising the participation and empowerment of the whole community? What factors might inhibit participation? What factors promote it? In particular, what effect do such factors have upon the development and integration of programmes that are gender-sensitive and seek to redress gender-based inequalities? These important questions will be returned to in chapters three and four.

Service provision: the technical perspective 2

The Kebkabiya project, when it was set up in 1985, had represented a change of focus from relief to development. But agencies must be ready to respond flexibly to changing needs, and for Oxfam Darfur much of 1988 was again dominated by relief needs, this time of tens of thousands of near-starving fugitives arriving from the civil war in South Sudan. This meant that the project took second place in the priorities of the Regional and Khartoum-based programme staff. Nevertheless, valuable work continued to be done, and the seedbanks proved to be a very successful method of increasing food security. After the rains, there was a need for some intensive work on formulating the future of the project.

Planning a second phase

Over the next few months meetings were held with both men and women in all of the centre villages where the seedbanks had been set up, and in a number of the outlying villages. The end result of this intensive process of community consultation was a proposal for a four-component second phase to the project (Strachan 1989). The activities in the second phase would include agricultural extension work, animal traction, animal health, and pest control. Two of the components, agricultural extension and animal health, would involve training workers chosen by the villagers, and these people would eventually be paid by the villagers for their services.

The increase in the scope of the programme activities required a new management structure, which was also discussed with the communities. It was decided that each village would elect representatives to a Village Centre Committee (VCC), which would replace the existing seedbank committees. These would meet in fourteen selected villages in the project area. Each of the fourteen VCCs would elect representatives to a Project Management Committee (PMC) which would meet in Kebkabiya town and which, together with the Oxfam staff, would decide the overall directions and strategy for the project.

Phase Two of the project began in earnest in the early months of 1989. The farthest sighted development, however, looking towards the eventual handover of the project and its management entirely to community control, was the registration of the PMC as a legally separate organisation representing the community side of the project. The legal processes were formally completed in November 1990 and the Kebkabiya Smallholders' Charitable Society (KSCS) was registered as a voluntary organisation with the Ministry of Social Affairs. The process of handover is described in chapter five.

Although the Kebkabiya project now consists of a multi-faceted programme which encompasses many community-based activities, such as education and literacy classes, the fundamental purpose still remains a technical one: to meet the identified needs of its members by successfully delivering a number of services and inputs to them which were not previously available. The community-based structures through which the project operates, and the acquiring of new technical and managerial skills by those involved in running it, evolved in response to those objectives. This chapter looks at the major technical components: why they were chosen, how they operate, their success, or otherwise, and their financial operating basis.

The seedbanks: a first step to enhancing food security

Oxfam's initial objective in response to the famine of 1984–85 had been to establish seedbanks to provide seed for farmers on rain-fed land. Although seeds were usually stored from the harvest for the next planting, the failed harvests and subsequent famine had forced people to eat the stored seeds.

The seedbank project represented a long-term contribution to food security rather than merely offering a one-off emergency donation to the communities. The principle of the seedbanks was radically different from the relief distributions of the immediate past, and the direct involvement of the community in the planning, construction, and management of the seedbank stores gave people a sense of control over and ownership of the project.

A seed bank is very similar to any other sort of bank in its basic operation. The user borrows not money but seed. Once this capital investment has brought a dividend in the form of a harvest, the loan is repaid to the bank, together with an extra amount. In Kebkabiya a loan of ten measuring bowls (*kora*) of seed will be repaid with eleven *kora* after the harvest. The extra amounts of seed then accumulate to provide a community reserve which can be held against lean years or, if it becomes too large to be stored without sustaining pest damage before it is required, can be sold for cash to raise money for other purposes.

Learning from experience

On a similar project in the neighbouring district of El Geneina, mistakes were made. In this instance, Oxfam failed to consult and involve local people in development activities. Instead of the community participating in initial plans, Oxfam staff themselves selected the villages in which seedbanks were to be built, and decided which areas the banks would cover. Arrangements were then made for the construction of the buildings where the seeds would be stored after repayment.

Outside labour was used and Oxfam brought in virtually all the materials that would be required, including water, sand, and cement. The speed with which the stores were erected, and the large populations that they would serve (over 10,000 people per store), meant that Oxfam learned little about the villages within which it was working. This comparative ignorance was mutual: the villagers had very little sense of ownership over what was happening and very little understanding of Oxfam's activities.

The principles of seed bank operation and community responsibility were never established, with the result that seeds distributed in 1985 in this area were not repaid to the seedbanks, and the committees formed to oversee the project never met. During fieldwork in 1987, villagers told Oxfam staff that they knew that the stores were supposed to be replenished and they were waiting for the Government to come to do so! It is clear from this experience that it takes time to build up a relationship of trust between an NGO and those it seeks to help. Unless the whole community is consulted, and involved in the planning and implementation of development activities, it is hard for people to feel a sense of responsibility. Nor is the community empowered, in any real sense of the word.

A different approach

The Kebkabiya team worked very differently. Two female staff members were given responsibility for setting up the project, and the first thing they did was to organise community meetings throughout the area, at which the 12 villages where seedbanks were to be constructed, the natural focal points for the communities concerned, were selected. The 12 seedbanks served a total population of about 30,000 — in contrast to the 80,000 people served from the seven in El Geneina. Because a smaller population was involved, a much closer relationship was made possible between Oxfam and the various communities.

Once the project area and the 'centres' within it had been defined, Oxfam's field officers tried to ensure not only that the villagers understood that they themselves were to manage the seed bank stocks, but also that they had the necessary skills to do so. The villagers were asked to demonstrate their commitment to the project by contributing water, sand, stones and, above all, labour, to construct the stores. Working more closely together, Oxfam staff and the villagers were able to learn more about each other and to establish the partnership that would be the hallmark of the project.

Not surprisingly, bearing in mind their past experiences of low levels of consultation from both government and foreign agencies, there was a strong element of initial scepticism from the villagers regarding Oxfam's rhetoric of participation. A member of one of the original seedbank committees remembers the village's first contacts with Oxfam:

> Radia and Nawal [Oxfam staff] held a meeting with us at which they explained the seedbank principle. It sounded like a good idea and we accepted it. They said they wanted our ideas but we didn't see it as consultation. After all, if someone offers you something you have to accept it, don't you? You don't argue with them.
>
> We discussed the division of responsibilities for constructing the seedbank store. Radia and Nawal proposed that we should provide labour and locally available materials such as sand and bricks. Oxfam would provide the cement, metal door, and roof and would arrange the transport of these materials. A lot of the representatives there argued that Oxfam as a rich foreign organisation should pay for everything, including labour; but in the end we accepted what they were suggesting. We weren't convinced by any particular argument that they put but it was obvious that Oxfam was refusing to offer anything more.

Villagers said later that, although at first they judged Oxfam against the background of their past experiences, they soon realised that the approach was different this time. There was extensive consultation before project work began, starting with contacts through the village sheikhs but widening beyond this. The regular visits from Oxfam staff helped to build a sense of trust and personal relationships with project staff. The principle of the seedbanks was different from the relief distributions of the immediate past; and the direct involvement of the community in the planning and construction of the seedbank stores gave an immediate sense of ownership over the project. Nevertheless, villagers had seen organisations come and go, and it took a number of years to build up the sense of trust and partnership that has characterised the later work of the project. The early seedbank committees followed the traditional pattern of village committees, but when the project moved into its second phase, the management committees became more democratic.

The seedbanks are now entirely under community control. The seedbank committees' ability to manage the operation was confirmed by a series of farsighted decisions taken after the excellent rains and harvest of 1988. Most committees decided that they would not be making loans during 1989 and would encourage their members to keep a personal stock of seed for the following years as well as repaying their loans. This meant that if the harvest was poor in 1989 — as was indeed the case — then there would be a reserve for 1990.

For some committees there was the additional problem of how to treat people whose crops had been destroyed during a locust infestation that struck the area during August. Here again, the management decisions were effective and creative, allowing people to re-schedule loans over the next few years, and with the seedbanks in the greatest overall difficulty as a result of attacks by locusts receiving support and assistance from those that could afford to offer it.

Seedbanks became the first of several success stories to come out of the Kebkabiya project and virtually everyone in the project area has used seedbanks, many on a regular basis.

Diversifying project goals

Throughout the first phase of the project, farmers had been pointing out to Oxfam staff that they were experiencing other problems. As a result, new project activities were undertaken in an *ad hoc* way during the first few years of the project's lifetime. These included the development of appropriate and affordable animal traction technology for the project area and agricultural extension work with farmers to improve soil and water conservation. There was also a demand for work in two other fields: animal health and pest control, and these were incorporated into the project's remit when a second phase was launched, following an extensive period of consultation with men and women in villages across the project area.

The project that failed

Before moving on to look at a number of the other successful technical interventions that have been developed in Kebkabiya we will pause to examine one instructive failure that was experienced in the early days.

At the same time as the seedbanks were being constructed and brought into operation, Oxfam was establishing a further project activity, also designed to reduce food insecurity. The contrast between the insecurity of the *goz* farmers in the rainfed sector and the relative affluence of those with access to *wadi* land that could be irrigated through times of poor rainfall had caught the imagination of some field staff. If *goz* farmers could be given access to *wadi* lands then their dependence upon unreliable rainfall would be diminished.

A brave but implausible experiment was then developed, with extension centres staffed by graduate advisers being established in five villages with access to *wadi* land. In each of these centres, groups of farmers comprising owners and non-owners of *wadi* land were formed to work the land cooperatively. The idea was that produce and profit would be shared between the providers of the land and the providers of the labour.

This cooperative approach, however, suffered a major failure in a vital technical area: the new method adopted to increase the water available for irrigation. Hand-dug wells lined with old oil drums were constructed from which water could be raised using a version of the Middle Eastern *shadoof*—a lifting device which balanced the water-bucket against a heavy weight at the end of a long fulcrum arm. But these new wells proved inefficient: the diameter of the drums made the wells too narrow, and because the drums were made of metal, water could not drain into the wells from the surrounding soil at a fast enough rate to enable them to be used continuously.

As well as these technical difficulties, the project suffered severe social problems. In setting up the project, far from adopting a participatory and consultative approach, Oxfam had sought to impose change in the established cultural relationships between *wadi* and *goz* farmers, without allowing the villagers involved any real say in the matter. Furthermore, by focusing attention on the owners of *wadi* land the project had moved away from its original intention of working with the poorest villagers and had started to establish a relationship with the wealthier cash-crop farmers that was to take several years to break off.

Alarm bells started to ring and an external consultancy was commissioned with a brief to consider Oxfam's relationships with the different groups of farmers. Concluding that the socio-economic differences between villages were of greater significance than the differences within them, the consultant recommended the reformulation of the project to focus upon 'farmers with insufficient resources to produce enough food to meet annual household requirements'. The reformulation exercise involved the most intensive and extensive consultation with the villagers that had been undertaken since the original setting up of the project. Starting from the premise that the farmers were the experts on agriculture in Darfur, their views were sought on the problems they actually experienced in food production. The views of village women were sought as well as those of the men. The project was thus reoriented away from technological towards social solutions. The aim would be to tackle poverty by challenging the marginalisation and subservience of the poor rather that attempt to change the technology of food production without looking at its sociology.

This failure by Oxfam to live up to its own ideals served to underline the importance of using participatory methods when planning projects. Field staff had allowed their enthusiasm for a superficially exciting technical and social innovation to override their commitment to this participation and consultation, and the result was a re-learning of the value of involving the community in project planning and implementation.

Service provision: the technical aspect

Animal traction

Animal traction was nothing new in Darfur and the farmers of Kebkabiya were well aware of how camels were used for agricultural work on the heavy alluvial soils of South Darfur and the *wadi* system around Kutum, to the north. The camel is a rich person's animal, indeed a sign of wealth in itself, and very few of Oxfam's beneficiaries had the opportunity to use camels on their farms. One of the project officers, Salih Abdel Mageed, was, however, beginning to explore the possibilities of using an animal which was much more widely owned among the poor — the donkey — for agricultural purposes.

Although similar work was being carried out on two large World Bank/European Community funded projects in South Darfur, a common reaction among the Kebkabiya farmers to the idea that a donkey might pull a plough, even through light *goz* soils, was one of utter incredulity. Salih worked slowly, purchasing implements from South Darfur and testing them on the Oxfam demonstration plots in the project area with a few local farmers who felt sufficient confidence in his judgement to take a risk with this new technology.

A crucial factor in the success of the project was to develop a plough especially designed to plough *goz* soils successfully and, once an appropriate design had been settled upon, to identify and train blacksmiths who could produce ploughs in sufficient quantities to meet the demand. Steel is imported into Sudan, and the price continually rises. To counter this problem, modifications to the design have been made, to use more wood in the construction of the plough, and to use steel only for the blade.

below Abdel Ahmed Ishaq and assistant working on an Oxfam plough, Kireiker village

25

Progress in this aspect of the Kebkabiya project has been slow to date, and demand for ploughs has outstripped supply. Of those interviewed in 1994, although the majority of knew about the scheme, only about a quarter had actually bought or used a plough, the majority of them men. Although locally trained blacksmiths are producing the special plough needed, a number of people complained that ploughs were not available in sufficient numbers. The most common reason given for not using this service, by women especially, was the cost of the implement — the rising cost of raw steel needed for plough manufacture has had to be passed on to the purchaser so that the initiative is sustainable.

Contour farming

Another success story of those early years was contour farming. Although the fields of most Kebkabiya farms, especially those on the plain, appear to be quite flat they are, of course, gently and imperceptibly sloped in random directions. This means that when rain falls much of it runs off the hard, dry soil surface before it has a chance to moisten the seeds beneath. As a year's rain may well fall in seven or eight distinct rainfall 'episodes', it is vital that maximum use is made of each episode.

The principle of contour farming is that seeds are not planted in a straight line up and down the field, but along the contours. The problem is to keep to the lines of contours when very often the slopes themselves are barely visible to the eye. The technique adopted was to construct a large wooden frame, perhaps five or six feet high, in the shape of a capital letter 'A'. A plumb-line would then be hung from its apex and the point at which it intersected the cross-bar when standing on a flat surface would be marked. This gave the position of the plumb-line when both feet of the frame were standing level with each other. One foot of the frame would then be placed in a corner of a field and the frame rotated around it until the plumb-line was again vertical. The position of the second foot would be marked on the ground and then the whole frame would be rotated around this foot until the original one was again on the ground with the plumb-line vertical. The third position would then be marked and the whole process repeated until the frame had been 'walked' in this manner across the whole field. The row of marked points would then all be on the same contour. This process would then be repeated several times down the field until the pattern of contours was clear.

The next stage was then to pull a rake, about three metres across and with nails hammered through it at half-metre intervals, along the lines of contour points so that the rows of dots were joined into continuous lines. The farmer would then plant his or her seeds along these lines and build a small furrow or

Service provision: th...

A Kireiker village demonstration plot compares donkey plough cultivation with hoe cultivation using both contour preparation and traditional straight line preparation.

top contour marking
centre planting hoe cultivated land
bottom donkey ploughing

ound' alongside the row of seeds so that when rain fell it would be directed along the contour and would penetrate down to the seeds rather than washing off the field and thus being of little benefit to the crop.

The idea was simplicity itself and very soon caught on across the project area. After the rains, especially in a poor year like 1987, there was a very clear difference between the fields that had been planted in straight lines and those that had been planted along the contours. It was a cheap, simple, and very effective technology that the farmers could control and pass on to others, and its success in the early years of the project helped very considerably to restore Oxfam's credibility with the farmers after the failure of the group-farming experiment. So successful did the technique prove that farmers in neighbouring villages, passing through the project area on their way to the Kebkabiya market, took up the technique on their own land, and contour farming spread rapidly throughout the area.

Animal health

Adapting a model used successfully by Oxfam in southern Sudan, the Kebkabiya project set up a training scheme for paravets to help to improve animal husbandry in the area. Paravets are analogous to community health workers in Primary Health Care programmes. Chosen by their own communities, they receive a short, practical training in animal health, building on indigenous knowledge, and introducing some simple preventive techniques. The training provided focused on the recognition of common diseases, the control of epidemics through vaccination, and the containment of diseases such as trypanosomiasis and pneumonia. Paravets are able to cover a wide area, and to give advice to farmers about animal health and nutrition. Their services are in great demand in their communities. They can obtain supplies of drugs from the project pharmacy.

Some of the paravets trained in Kebkabiya are female. Rogaya Yusif of Dadi centre, for example, was given a series of four training sessions by the Oxfam veterinary officer, covering recognition of animal diseases, use of drugs, and practical skills such as giving injections:

> ❬ As well as treating sick animals I also do training sessions for the villagers in birthing techniques and preventive health care for their animals. Usually people come to my home if their animals are sick, but if they are too ill to be brought I will go to them. If I can't diagnose the problem myself then I'll refer them to the KSCS vet in Kebkabiya. Usually it's the men who come with the animals, but women who are heads of households also bring animals. I think these women would also

have brought sick animals if the centre had selected a male paravet, but the project helps them particularly by making services available locally and by allowing them drugs on credit. The project has given access to veterinary services to many people who didn't have it before. **’**

below Rogaya Yusif Ahmed, a paravet in Dadi village

Revolving funds: the economic basis for the projects

The use of revolving funds evolved as the major vehicle for all resource mobilisation. If a project is to become sustainable, rather than requiring constant subsidies or grants, the initial grant must be regarded as a loan, and repaid so that it can be re-used to benefit others. Getting a revolving fund system to work was not, however, without its problems in Sudan.

The first funds were established in early 1987 with an initial allocation of LS14,000 (then worth about £3,100) for the sale of seeds. Hussein Abdallah was the Project Officer responsible for the administration of these funds:

‘ People were reluctant to repay their loans because it was a new idea and they didn't understand the objective. This was gradually overcome by involving the seedbank committees in the management of the funds. At first their role was to decide what quantities of each type of seed to buy and they could see that if the loans weren't repaid then there was less money to spend on seeds in following years. Later on, in 1989, the committees became involved in the pricing policy for the seeds and we began to involve them in the actual purchasing, taking committee members with us so that they could become familiar with the places from which we got the seeds. The problems of non-repayment and occasional embezzlement have now disappeared. *

This demonstrates the importance of ensuring that the principles behind a development intervention are discussed fully, particularly when the method adopted is an unfamiliar one. It can take a long time to build up a relationship of trust between all those involved. In one case the impasse was resolved by a personal visit from the Kebkabiya Shertai, Adam Ahmedai, who explained the principle of the seedbank to villagers and put his personal authority behind the concept. The villagers were prepared to place a degree of trust in their traditional leader that they were not yet willing to extend to a foreign agency, and the loans were repaid.

Coping with inflation

The revolving funds ran into serious problems when inflation began to accelerate in 1990 and 1991. The project had to price ahead of inflation in order to try and preserve the value of the funds, which brought complaints from the farmers that such forward-pricing policies made the seeds more expensive than in Kebkabiya market! Pricing was therefore pegged to reflect the cost of seeds in the market, with the result that funds began to lose their real value. Faced with a choice between funds not being used or losing their real value, a management decision was taken to allow the funds to run down.

However, the farmers, anxious to retain the security provided by the funds, fought for a compromise pricing policy to be adopted by the PMC. This new policy allowed for some increase in prices to be made, to reflect inflationary pressures, but not to such an extent that villagers were prevented from using the funds. Although this slowed down the fund's loss of value, and other measures were introduced, such as purchasing seed as soon as funds were available, rather than holding repayments in cash, the situation was not sustainable. As Sudan moved to the brink of hyper-inflation in 1992, the farmers were simply unable to bear the full inflation figure.

Oxfam helped by topping up the funds with supplementary grants and, when a major purchase of seeds of a new drought-resistant sorghum variety was made from Kordofan, the proceeds from their sale to farmers was added to the funds. By late 1992, the value of funds was in excess of LS100,000, but in real terms this was worth less than the original LS14,000 in 1987.

As the project moved into its second phase, the revolving fund mechanism was used for a variety of new purposes. The supply of veterinary drugs, animal fodder, animal traction inputs, and pest control materials, and the organisation of women's projects were all based on the same principle. The total value of all the revolving funds in 1996 had grown to LS5,800,000, though this figure mainly reflects the effects of inflation: the total hard currency value of the funds being only around £25,159.

Veterinary drugs and the pharmacy

The most successful of the revolving funds has been the one used for veterinary drugs, but even this requires constant and skilful adjustment by those managing it. The majority of drugs are purchased locally from El Fasher and only a small amount is added to their wholesale purchase cost, usually in the region of 10–15 per cent. Other drugs are purchased in Khartoum and, with Oxfam paying the transport costs directly, up to 50 per cent of the purchase cost can be saved. In addition, an annual bulk order is purchased from the UK and, here too, enormous savings on costs can be made. The purchases from Khartoum and the UK thus cross-subsidise local purchases enabling a pricing structure that allows the drugs to be sold at prices below those of commercial pharmacies and yet still return a profit to the project.

In 1994 the revolving drug funds were consolidated into a self-financing community pharmacy, based in the KSCS offices. The project's paravets have a credit allowance from the pharmacy while herders from outside the project area can purchase drugs over the counter after first consulting KSCS's vet. These direct sales are not allowed to exceed 25 per cent of turn-over, which

below A community veterinary pharmacy

ensures that supplies are always available for the community paravets. The pharmacy is managed by a committee consisting of three PMC members and three members of staff, and prices are reset on a monthly basis taking into account a survey of prices in the commercial veterinary pharmacies in Kebkabiya. A comparative survey of prices in the KSCS pharmacy with those in the market showed that the pharmacy is indeed able to keep its prices below those of commercial traders by working to lower profit margins.

ITEM	MARKET	KSCS
Drugs		
Tetramycin	1500	1400
Ivomec	20000	17000
Antycide	2700	2975
Pamizole powder	14000	11500
Pamizole tablets	7500	3500
Eye infection cream	200	340
Gamatox	20200	20000
Tetramizole powder	6500	5000

The pharmacy was expecting to make a profit of about LS7,256,000 in its first year: approximately £11,267 at late-1994 exchange rates. It is hoped that the veterinary component, at least, will be self-financing, with the profit covering the salaries of the KSCS vet and his assistant and those of the community paravets.

Although this fund escapes the problem faced by agriculturalists in that demand for drugs is constant rather than seasonal, there are still challenges to be faced. One of these is the time it takes to turn around revenue, resulting in large amounts of cash being held before a further purchase is made. The current inflation rate is now stated officially as 56 per cent, but independent analysts put the rate far higher at around 80 per cent. Whatever the exact inflation rate, purchasing power is being lost all the time.

To avoid this problem, commercial veterinary pharmacists make weekly trips to markets at Kutum and Mellit, where trucks with consignments of drugs arrive from Libya almost daily. However, there are dangers in obtaining drugs in this way, because such drugs may be contraband or, as there is no quality control, even fake, which is a common occurrence. As bulk purchases have to be pre-paid, embezzlement of deposited funds is also a constant problem. The higher profit margins of the market pharmacists are designed in part to cover these risks.

The viability of revolving funds

The problems for the other revolving funds are even greater. As purchases of most inputs are seasonal, farmers cannot be expected to repay loans before they have brought in a harvest which represents a return on their investment. Loans are therefore usually outstanding for periods of three to six months, during which time their real value drops drastically. Although it was agreed by the programme that 15 per cent was a realistic administration figure to put on top of the amount loaned, this does not cover inflation. Even here there are areas of uncertainty due to the Islamic prohibition on the charging of interest (though, in effect, Islamic banks do charge rates of up to 38 per cent on short-term loans). Service and administrative charges were also incorporated but farmers were far from convinced about adding in these charges, arguing that Oxfam pays the organisational overheads anyway.

At the present time, with additional proposals for a credit scheme to be established within the women's component of the programme, project staff are working on a number of creative ideas for cash credit to overcome this problem. These in due course will be put to the KSCS Project Management Committee for consideration. One idea is to value loans in terms of a 'hard' commodity whose price is familiar to villagers, such as soap. The amount to be repaid would be linked to the prevailing cost of the numbers of bars of soap's worth of money originally borrowed.

Such ideas notwithstanding, there is no realistic solution in sight for the major revolving funds while Sudan's inflation rate remains at current levels. The primary objective of the funds is to make inputs available to farmers and this means that prices must remain below those of the commercial market for the actual goods or for comparable items where the project is offering new technologies such as the donkey ploughs. For the foreseeable future it appears that Oxfam will have to continue subsidising the revolving funds.

Any attempt to make them self-financing is likely to run counter to the objective of making resources available at affordable prices to the poorest farmers. This means that total self-sufficiency for the project is likely to remain an impossible ideal, because the economic environment within which local management decisions have to be taken is subject to the influence of negative factors, such as inflation, operating at national and international levels. The implications of this, and other external and internal factors, for the KSCS's long-term viability and growth, will be looked at in a later chapter.

Empowering communities

top An executive committe meeting of the Kebkabiya Smallholders' Charitable Society (KSCS)
bottom A seedbank in Debli village

Involving the community 3

In the previous chapters, giving an account of the evolution and activities of the Kebkabiya project, the importance of involving the community in decision making has been constantly emphasised. Participation is an essential aspect of community development, and in the case of the Kebkabiya project, was vital if responsibility for the project was eventually to be handed over to the community. We will now look at the way in which the idea of representational democracy and accountability was developed in the management of project activities.

The seedbank committees

Although, as we saw in the first chapter, a variety of forms of social representation existed among the Kebkabiya communities before Oxfam's involvement in the area, traditional village councils tended to be male-dominated and composed of members of the more influential local families. The nature of the seedbank project meant that a more participatory and accountable structure was necessary and that members who were willing to learn financial, administrative, and managerial skills would be required. A system was thereby established under which each village using a particular seedbank would send a representative to the seedbank committee which met in the 'centre' village, the village in which the seedbank was physically located. Once established, each committee essentially worked as a separate unit, though the committee chairmen (for they were exclusively male) did meet together at the Oxfam office to discuss issues of wider concern such as the need for replenishing of seed stocks after the widespread harvest failure in 1987. As the project moved towards new activities a formal Project Management Committee (PMC) was established comprising the Oxfam staff on the project and the chairmen of the twelve seedbank committees.

A complete handover of the seedbanks to village control came as the outcome of a process rather than as a carefully planned event. As the committees gained in confidence they were taking more and more decisions on their own and there was simply less and less for Oxfam staff to do. Monitoring of repayments became a redundant process as the villagers accepted the idea that they had a community resource to safeguard. The decision in virtually all centres to make no loans, apart from exceptional cases, after the outstanding harvest of 1988, demonstrated the ability of the committees to manage the scheme wisely.

The Phase Two project proposal in 1989 thus saw no role for Oxfam in the day-to-day management of the seed banks (Strachan, 1989). However, it did call for the creation of a central seedbank in Kebkabiya. This central reserve was designed to provide a solution to the problem of localised crop failures in a few centres; such failures resulted in Oxfam having to restock each affected centre. The central seedbank, now stocked from centres which had experienced a surplus harvest, not only enhanced the overall security of the seed supply, but would be able to undertake distribution of seeds to 'centre' banks that had suffered crop failures. The banks were now linked within a system that spread risk more evenly, by balancing supply against demand over a wide area, and which was therefore more sustainable.

A central seed bank nevertheless required a considerable exercise of trust, as ultimate control over distribution now lay not in local committees but with the PMC, meeting in Kebkabiya. The fact that such a change was, by and large, accepted is a measure of how far the villagers had changed in their attitudes towards the project since the days when foreign agencies had simply been seen as sources of free hand-outs to be taken while they lasted.

The Village Centre Committees (VCCs)

The seedbank committees began to take on a number of extra responsibilities during the first phase of the project, such as the organisation of training in contour farming and animal traction technologies, and the supervised management of revolving funds for the purchase and distribution of cash-crop seeds. The second phase of the project then consolidated the various priority requests that had been raised with Oxfam staff by the seedbank committees and, following extensive consultation, a more formalised system of community accountability was proposed.

As well as recognising the changed role of the committees, the restructuring of the system for community accountability sought to address the problem of the male domination of the committees. Established in a hurry in the immediate aftermath of the 1984–5 famine they had inevitably reflected the power structures of the village communities themselves, and the patriarchal nature of Sudanese society. Increasingly women had come to feel disenfranchised or even ignored by the project.

The committees that had run the twelve seed banks were now replaced by Village Centre Committees (VCCs). Each village served by the centre would elect two representatives, one male and one female, to the VCC, which would meet in the central seedbank villages. Each of the sixteen VCCs — four more villages were now added to the list — would elect a male and a female representative to the PMC which would continue to meet in Kebkabiya town and, together with the Oxfam staff, would decide the overall directions and strategy for the project.

Village Extension Agents (VEAs)

In addition to the paravets discussed in the previous chapter, each VCC would also select a villager to be trained as a Village Extension Agent (VEA) by Oxfam staff in the technical agricultural skills relating to the project such as contour farming, use of new varieties, pest-control methods, and animal traction techniques. Training courses for VEAs and paravets, run by project staff, were started in 1989. VEAs represent the technical and logistical link of the project with villages, initiating training, meeting the demands of the members, dealing with allocations and complaints, and collecting repayments of loans.

A good insight into some of the day-to-day problems faced by the VEAs was given by Eisa Mohammed of Mailu centre in the foothills of the Jebel Marra:

> *The inputs available are not always enough to meet the demand from farmers and there are then problems with deciding how to allocate what is available. Although the centre committee decides on the allocations policy I often have to face the complaints of those who are disappointed. For instance, this year there was a shortfall in the cash-crop seeds available. The committee decided to allocate according to the size of farm that people had so that those with more land got more seed. I then had to field the complaints of those who felt that equal rather than proportionate amounts should have been given to everyone.*
>
> *The problem is made worse by the fact that it's often difficult to get people to repay the loans they have had. If the centre's outstanding loans are more than a certain amount then the amount of extra seed I can take on credit from Kebkabiya is restricted. I have to report this to the committee and let them chase up the defaulters but everyone suffers in the interim because of the credit limit placed on the centre.*

The VEAs are now accountable to the Agricultural Officer employed by KSCS. The Society's approach continues to emphasise the community development aspects of the VEA role over the technical, and puts the VEAs at the forefront of its activities.

Women's participation in village committees

The women spoken to during the consultation exercise which was carried out in order to shape the second phase of the project reported very little understanding of the project and had received little benefit from it. In considering ways in which this situation might be rectified, there were considerable debates about the best way to involve women in the project. Some women felt that they would never be taken seriously in mixed meetings and that their interests would be best represented through separate women's committees. Other women felt that separate female committees would be collectively ignored and so would marginalise women's position even further. In the end, it was decided that women in each centre should decide for themselves how they wished to be represented. In all but two of the centres they opted for separate committees; in the two exceptions, more outspoken women could be counted upon to speak up for the other women.

The women on the committees, whichever model was decided upon in their centre, were supported by two new Oxfam staff members. These were high-school women graduates with a bilingual knowledge of Fur and Arabic, and a community development background. In addition to enhancing the confidence and competence of the female representatives on the committees, their role was also to ensure that the voice of the women in the villages was heard at the PMC, meeting in Kebkabiya, which many of the women from the remoter villages in particular were unable to attend.

The Kebkabiya Smallholders' Charitable Society (KSCS)

Although the PMC, despite its name, started off in effect as a body to be consulted by the Oxfam staff who, at that time, still largely controlled and managed the activities of the project, it began to take on more and more power and responsibility. This power was formalised in the creation of the Kebkabiya Smallholders' Charitable Society (KSCS), registered with the Ministry of Social Welfare as a voluntary organisation in late 1990. It is a membership organisation with a monthly membership fee of ten Sudanese pounds (later raised to LS20 — approx 3p) per household. The members elect VCC representatives. The PMC remained the supreme decision-making body, but the regular work of the Society would be conducted by a smaller Executive Committee. This new status as a registered voluntary organisation enables the KSCS to undertake its own fund raising, hold budgets, and employ staff. In time, KSCS would take over the management of project activities from Oxfam, but this would be a gradual process, with responsibility for managing various components of the project being transferred over a period of time. The process of handover will be described in chapter five.

A constitutional workshop held in 1992 determined the current format of the Society's system of community accountability. The constitution formalised the representational structure of the Oxfam-managed project, with each village sending two representatives (one male and one female) to a VCC which in turn sends one man and one woman to the PMC. The PMC itself meets every three months and one of its functions is to elect an Executive Committee (EC) of ten people on a post-by-post basis — at least four of whom must be women. The EC itself meets at least once a month.

Under this revised constitution, the PMC is now the ultimate legislative body of the organisation, though it is accountable to an Annual General Assembly of all VCC members. The EC is the executive branch of the KSCS, implementing policy determined by the PMC, and managing staff.

How was KSCS created?

The fact that an eventual handover would be the logical outcome for the project was realised from the very earliest days of the PMC. Soon after the PMC's formation in 1989, a working party was established to recommend the most appropriate route for independent registration of the project. Enquiries were made of the Ministry of Agriculture, the Union of Co-operatives, and the Ministry of Social Welfare and the PMC eventually accepted that the most appropriate route to a handover was through registration as a voluntary society with the Ministry of Social Welfare. This decision recognised that the main purpose of the Kebkabiya project was social development with an emphasis on targeting the poorest people in the community. Staff of the Ministry confirmed that the broad objectives were compatible with those of the Ministry and the PMC set about drafting a constitution. This was completed over a period of about six months and the Society was registered in November 1990.

Under the constitution, the objectives and methods of the Society are defined as follows:

Objectives

1 To develop the abilities of local farmers and to protect them from exploitation.
2 To develop local economic and social groups.
3 To work for the development of vulnerable groups in the local community such as women and children.
4 To develop the agricultural, livestock husbandry and other traditional skills of local individuals and groups.
5 To raise awareness of co-operative activities that will lead to the improvement and conservation of soil, water, range and pasture, and forestry resources and of the local environment generally.
6 To contribute to social and cultural development.
7 To advance the development of rural women.

Empowering communities

8 To assist people affected by natural and man-made disasters.

9 To work towards the unity of all the people in the Society.

10 To work towards equitable gender relations.

Methods

1 To mobilise local and external financial resources for the use of rehabilitation, development and emergency projects.

2 To implement activities that will provide services for the individuals and communities within the project area.

3 To raise the awareness of individuals and groups through extension and consciousness-raising activities.

4 To contribute to the provision of agricultural and livestock services, seed and cereal banks and credit schemes.

5 To ensure the participation of villagers in the planning and management of all the Society's activities.

6 In implementing any activities, the following points should always be borne in mind:

a) the highest priority will always be given to the poorest households

b) to ensure the self-reliance of the local community, especial use will be made of their agricultural and livestock herding knowledge and their developmental skills.

c) the Society will always seek the fullest participation of local beneficiary communities at all stages of planning, implementing, monitoring and evaluating projects.

7 The Society's activities will be closely co-ordinated with the development policies of local and central government.

8 There will be the closest possible co-ordination with parastatal corporations, institutes, government operational ministries, voluntary organisations and local and national NGOs.

9 KSCS will seek to build relationships with governmental departments and national and international NGOs in order to further its objectives.

A question of accountability

The pyramidal structure of the KSCS means that decisions affecting the lives of around 65,000 people are taken by 32 people: a ratio of about 1:2030. This raises major questions about how accountable this body is, and how effectively it represents all its constituents.

The first thing to note is that PMC members are often not elected at all in the formal sense of the word. Many representatives have actually been selected by consensus decisions in VCC centres. The delegates to these centres are themselves selected by meetings that take place within their own villages, though the fact that the meetings are held in open session means that the representatives from surrounding villages may be outnumbered by casual attenders from the centre village where the meetings are held. Several of the representatives have also reported having faced no opposition at their selection, and some of them were unclear as to why their names had been put forward in the first place. There is also considerable variation as to how members perceive their role.

At one extreme, a female representative to the PMC of two years' standing stated that she did not know why her name had been put forward though she assumed it to be due to the fact that she had served on now defunct village committees during the period of the Nimeiri regime in the early 1980s. She said that she did not always know when a meeting was due to be held and could not always attend anyway as she had no donkey and the walk to Kebkabiya took two to three hours. She had only attended three PMC meetings and she did not really understand what they were about. This may be due to the fact that she understands Arabic only with difficulty: although summary translations into Fur are available at the meetings, the bulk of the business is conducted in Arabic. Her understanding of her role was that she was to reflect the views of village women, to receive and distribute inputs, and to collect the money owed by village women to Oxfam.

> ❝ Often the men get things from the project and I'm not informed about what's happening. I'm kept in the dark about many things to do with the project. I don't ask what's going on and I don't expect that I'd be told if I did. People would say that I wasn't being respectful. ❞

Although she had been offered places on training courses to do with the project she had not attended them. From her perspective, she had received little from the project and didn't think that the project had done much for women. However, her views did not seem to be borne out by other women in the same centre, and even in the same village, and it is difficult to escape the conclusion that her appointment and retention as women's representative reflected the fact that a very low value was placed on the role of the female representative in that centre.

Interestingly, people from her village said that if they had an issue to raise with the project they would take it up through the centre's paravet, an influential man from the same village, the stock-keeper at the seedbank store or the male centre representative, himself from a different village.

At the opposite end of the scale of involvement is Adam Sayed, male representative for Segering centre:

> The post of the village representative to the committee in Segering had been vacant for some time after the death of the previous member when I was asked to take it. I was appointed at a general meeting of the village — there was no vote and I was the only nominee.
>
> I don't know exactly why they chose me but I've lived in the village all my life and used to be on the Rural Council too, so I suppose that had something to do with it. I know that the consultation process is essential to the working of the project and ensures that it meets the real needs that we experience. I'm responsible for attending the PMC meetings four times a year and for raising requests from this centre at those meetings. After the meetings I tour the villages in this centre and meet with their two representatives to make sure they know what's happening and to get any feedback from them.
>
> I also meet with the paravet and the VEA regularly — they report to me in the first instance. I understand the objectives of the project but I don't get a lot of information about its broader workings. Anyway, I see my role as being to represent the interests of these villages. We [the PMC] have elected an Executive Committee to carry on the detailed workings of the project.

Exercising choice

If PMC members are only partially representative of their centres, another way to gauge the accountability of the council system is in how easy it is for constituents to deselect a representative who is not performing well. Women in the village of Bora complained that they had got very little out of the project but rejected possible explanations for this that had to do with their social marginalisation in the community, material poverty, language difficulties or the weight of other domestic and food production tasks. Their explanation was simple:

> Our representative was hopeless. For a long time we thought that Oxfam was simply not delivering inputs to the centre but gradually we realised that she was not doing anything to find out about it or to tell us. It is true that this went on for years, but this is how things work in the villages. We don't expect things to happen quickly and we give a person time to prove themselves and deliver. Once we realised the true source of the problem we got rid of her and elected a replacement. But this was only earlier this year so there hasn't been time for the situation to improve for us.

Involving the community

If the learning process in the workings of a democratic structure is a long one, there is at least an interim solution for villagers in that they have a number of other channels through which they can raise project issues apart from through the formal structures of the project's system of popular representation.

In centres and villages where the representatives seemed to be least active, farmers suggested many other channels through which they could raise problems and requests for inputs. These included project staff in the villages such as paravets, village extension agents and storekeepers, traditional authorities such as the sheikhs, centre representatives when these came from other villages, and direct approaches to Oxfam and KSCS staff and Executive Committee members either when they were in Kebkabiya for the twice-weekly market or when they visited their villages.

Such approaches may help to protect the Society's own credibility and to prevent villagers becoming disillusioned with the lack of services received, but might also serve to undermine the democratic foundations of the KSCS.

Perhaps the greatest hope for the long-term democratic approach is the evidence that many of the people in the villages feel that the project offers them a voice, but that if they do not use it then they cannot expect to benefit from what it has to offer:

> If we just sit here and wait we can't expect people to come up and give us things. (Woman in Somati village)

> I had to be in El Fasher to attend to a sick relative when the pasta-making machines arrived. My deputy didn't do anything about requesting one for this centre so we missed our chance. If we don't ask for ourselves we can only expect others to get in first.
> (PMC member, Kireiker)

> The key people in ensuring that we benefit are the centre representatives. If they don't tell the village representatives what is being distributed then we won't get anything — they have to call the village representatives together regularly so that they know what's going on and can tell us. (Woman in Um Raob village).

It seems that the success of the KSCS will eventually hinge upon whether or not enough members in the community decide that only by becoming involved themselves can they really increase control over their own lives. As the Executive Officer for Kebkabiya Area Council, the senior civil servant in the District, put it:

> The people have been given drugs and seeds, but the most important thing is training. When Oxfam has to leave, the community will have

been trained to carry on the work. The independence they have been given will eventually give them a full sense of self-identity because real development is the development of the person. **)**

In the next chapter, we will consider how far that full sense of self-identity through project participation has been realised by women.

The threat of insecurity

Throughout the lifetime of the project in Kebkabiya, civil insecurity in the area has posed a recurring threat to local communities and sometimes brought project activities to a halt. Two major tribal conflicts — between the Fur and the Arabs in 1988-9 and between the Arabs and the Zaghawa in 1994 — have affected the area, and there has been a constant backdrop of armed banditry linked at least in part to the civil war in neighbouring Chad. The deaths of two members of the project's staff — Abdel Moneim Abakora in 1987 and Ebada Abdel Gabbar in 1993 — as a result of this insecurity has brought its effects to the very forefront of the project's attention. A number of VCC representatives have also lost their lives in the tribal fighting and in 1992 the Chair of the Daya committee, Ibrahim Adam, on his way to Kebkabiya with revolving fund money, was murdered by bandits who attacked him and stole the money.

Daya, deep in the Jebel Si mountains, is one of the project centres that has been worst affected. The road between Daya and Kebkabiya, which takes almost two hours to travel by Landrover and at least eight by donkey, winds up and down through the mountain passes, where travellers are vulnerable to ambush. The villagers of the Daya area are in no doubt about the effect of the insecurity on the project and the centre's paravet, Sadiq Ahmed, described the measures that he and his fellow villagers have taken to counter the problem:

> **(** It's had a serious effect upon my work. The road to Kebkabiya has been cut off by bandits or by fighting on numerous occasions. When we can't use the road we get to Kebkabiya through the mountains by using little-known footpaths that are too narrow and steep even to take a donkey along. This means that we have to carry the veterinary drugs back to the village on our own backs. Of course they're heavy so the amount we can bring has to be limited to the most essential. Even then we are afraid that we might be attacked specifically for the drugs, which are a valuable commodity. The mountain route to Kebkabiya takes two days to walk. We set off at about 4 a.m. and arrive in Kebkabiya around sunset the day after, though if we believe that there are bandits in the immediate area we travel mainly by night. **)**

A similar story was told by Mohammed Ahmed Salih, who replaced Ibrahim Adam on the PMC after his murder:

> ❛ The insecurity hasn't prevented us from getting to Kebkabiya, even after Ibrahim was killed. If you are chosen by your community to do a job for them then you must fulfil that responsibility. If I hadn't continued to carry out my job then the whole area would have been deprived of the services of the project and would have lost the benefit from them. For this reason we've done everything we can to keep the project going, travelling at night and using back routes to Kebkabiya whenever the road has been unsafe. ❜

At the other end of the project area, in the foothills of the Jebel Marra, project activities came close to closure during the Fur-Arab conflict of 1988–9. At least one project village was razed to the ground and a number of committee representatives lost their lives in the fighting. The Chair of the Debli committee, Mohammed Fadul Siri, relates a narrow escape:

> ❛ I was riding to Kebkabiya carrying a lot of money as I was going to buy sugar for the village as well as take the revolving fund money to Oxfam. I knew that there were armed bands around so I'd gone on horse-back. As I turned a corner in the road I found my way blocked by an armed man on camel-back. Hoping that he hadn't seen me I quickly turned the horse around but found that my retreat was blocked by another — it was an ambush. There was no other course but to flee and I managed to escape from them as they fired shots around me. Had I gone to Kebkabiya that day by donkey I wouldn't be here to tell you the story now. ❜

The determination of the villagers of the Daya and Debli areas to keep the project going in the face of such extreme problems provides perhaps the ultimate testimony to its value to their community. People may attend meetings out of curiosity or elect representatives to gain some marginal benefits from a project; they are highly unlikely to put their lives in immediate danger unless there are very powerful reasons indeed for doing so.

Empowering communities

above Salih Abdel Mageed (UK project coordinator) and Halima Noor (handmills coordinator) discuss the introduction of handmills with the women of Somati village

Participation and gender 4

In chapter one, we briefly looked at the global characteristics of gender relations, and at gender relations within the Kebkabiya project area. In this chapter we take a closer look at the issues, and consider the influence that the system of beliefs and values within society with regard to the social roles and relationships of men and women had upon women's use of the project's resources, and their participation in its running.

The sexual division of labour

In most rural communities in Africa, women's productive work such as agricultural labour or petty trading is perceived largely as an extension of their household activities. These activities usually, in themselves, have little perceived economic or social value: they are not seen as 'real' work, but as part of the 'natural' roles that women perform. Women's activities are considered to have less cultural and social value than those performed by men. In this way, not only are large parts of women's work ignored, but their activities and influence are seen as belonging to the private sphere of the family and household. In other words, the importance of the work changes according to whether it is done by women or men.

The outer public sphere of commerce, trade and decision making is restricted almost exclusively to men, though of course this can vary from culture to culture, and from one economic and social group to another. Men also provide the bridge between the private and public spheres of society, and with the wider world outside the community. Women in general are perceived, and perceive themselves, as having less social and economic value, in every respect, than men.

'The tools of men'

The traditional view of women in the Kebkabiya area has been summed up by the Executive Officer as: 'women were men's assets; they were tools for men to do with as they wished'. Early attempts by project staff to reach women made, at best, minor inroads into such deeply held patriarchal beliefs. Women themselves had correspondingly few expectations that they would or should be involved, regarding any such aspiration as both unseemly and a time-consuming irrelevance.

Men took all community decisions and represented their village to outsiders. Although a small minority of villages had had women on the committees set up to administer government supplies of sugar, a clearly domestic, and thus a household concern, it was exceptionally rare for women to be involved in governmental committees. Apart from such obvious social and economic constraints which adversely influenced women's participation, there were other reasons why a majority of women failed to get involved. Lack of time, low educational attainment, and physical distance were significant factors which prevented women from participating.

Barriers to women's participation

The workload faced by women is daunting. They have water to fetch, homes to keep clean, grain to grind, meals to cook, firewood to chop and carry, children and other dependents to care for, as well as fields to cultivate and animals to look after. They had little time to get involved in planning a project. Any activity that included simply sitting around and talking was seen as a task for men.

Women's educational levels are also much lower than those of men. Although many village men are illiterate, even more village women cannot read or write. Their lack of contact with the world beyond the village also means that the majority of the women in Fur villages can not speak Arabic — the language of government and aid agencies — with any degree of fluency. A man who cannot speak Arabic is a rarity, as is a Fur village woman who can.

The distance from a village to a VCC meeting also greatly influenced some women's decisions not to become involved. Lack of a donkey — a common means of transport — meant that attendance at a meeting might entail walking for up to two hours to get to it. In all, five or six hours of a woman's time might be spent in getting to and from, and attending, a meeting. To many women, this was not a realistic proposition.

Turning theory into practice

The problem of how to include women in the development process was one that occupied Oxfam staff from the outset of the project. One tempting solution was to isolate women into a single group. In practical development terms women often do need to be specially targeted, but such emphasis can lead to women being perceived in isolation, somehow outside the main — male — society, not an integral part of it.

Oxfam's approach would be that women, men, and children, should not be viewed in isolation from one another, but as interdependent. Any change in existing gender roles that seeks to encourage more egalitarian attitudes within a society represents a challenge to existing power relations, and, in so doing, affects every member of that society. Development agencies who seek to involve women in projects can act from rather different motives: from a desire to promote equity and to ensure that women and men benefit from the project to the same extent, or from a belief that for a community to move in the direction of gender equity is a form of development, to be promoted as an end in itself.

However, without a holistic analysis of social relations, projects targeted at women to redress their inequality can in fact increase their workloads, alienate them from their society, and expose them to forceful reactions from men who feel their 'given' place within society is under threat. Despite the fact that many of the staff and consultants involved in the early days of the Kebkabiya project were women, committed to a gender-sensitive approach to development, bringing about a change in women's status in their communities, after centuries of female exclusion from decision-making, was to prove hard to realise in practice.

Even during fieldwork leading to the formulation of the second-phase project proposals in 1989, a female project officer — one of those who had set the project up in the first place — reported that women were still saying they had little idea of how the project worked. For almost four years they had seen Landrovers driving in and out of their village but had no real conception of what their occupants were doing there; nor did they think it was their place to be asking about it.

Early attempts to include women

Throughout the first few years of the project Oxfam grappled constantly with the problem of involving women in the project. The speed with which the seed banks had to be established as part of a post-famine rehabilitation exercise could not be allowed to prevent community participation in the fundamental decisions and planning exercises.

Female participation in the planning of the seed banks was largely confined to joining in construction work. This hardly challenged established gender roles, as unskilled labour on building sites is often carried out by women in western Sudan, as in other poor countries.

Once the seedbanks were up and running, Oxfam staff continued to try to persuade women to become members of the management committees, but with very limited success. The committees had been established on a largely male-only basis during the famine months and it was virtually impossible to attempt to get women included in what on the surface of things was a successful arrangement. Project staff therefore concentrated their efforts on making sure that women knew that seed was available for loan to them. As a result, of all the services offered by the project, the seedbanks would appear at the present time to be the project service best understood and most widely used by the village women.

When the seedbank committees began to diversify into the management of revolving funds for the purchase and distribution of improved and new varieties of cash-crop seeds, Oxfam staff used this as another opportunity to draw women into the management of the project. Men were happier to have women involved in this new service, perhaps for no other reason than that the task may have seemed rather irksome to them. Project staff found that women often made better fund-managers than men, being more realistic in their projections and considerably more reluctant to get into debt.

The abortive experiment of basing graduate extension workers in villages to promote cooperative farming had the potential to help Oxfam to build bridges to women in the five villages in which the programme worked. However, the extent to which this happened was wholly dependent upon the approach of the individual extensionist. In one extension village the current women's representative stated that it was a sense of anger at the fact that the extensionist did not do any work with them that spurred women into demanding involvement in subsequent phases.

Elsewhere, however, the story was different. One female extension worker, together with a male extension worker and his wife, began to build a sense of trust with the women in the two centres where they worked. The women became regular visitors to their homes and through such visits, they became familiar with project activities and objectives. Even though the use of village extension workers was eventually abandoned, the rapport established paid dividends in later stages of the project.

Extension training

After the village extension worker programme was dropped, the remaining staff on the project worked hard to secure the participation of women in their extension training sessions, which focused largely on the technique of contouring. To encourage women to participate further, each centre now had an 'extension group' of two men and two women, who attended all the practical training sessions and then passed on their skills to other villages served by the centre.

Unfortunately, the security and staffing constraints facing the project at that time meant that the programme had to be confined to five centres. Even so, there were still complaints from some of the female villagers that men's land was given a higher priority than that of women when it came to selecting fields for contouring by the community during the dry season. Men, it was claimed, were able to exert greater pressure on the organisers to get their fields included and so were assisted first. This issue still remains hotly contested, and unresolved, even today.

Integration or separate development?

As we saw in chapter two, there was a lot of debate about whether the Village Centre Committees (VCCs) should take the form of two committees — one for men and one for women — or a combined committee of male and female representatives. The argument on one side was that women would be inhibited from speaking out in mixed committees; on the other, that a separate female structure would be marginalised and would become a disempowered shadow of the men's structure.

In the event, in all but two centres, the women opted for separate committees. Over the next year or so women got used to having a collective voice and discussing and analysing their problems together. Gradually they became convinced that even if they did work out problems within their group, it was of no value to them unless they were heard and taken seriously by the men of their community. During the period of the separate committees, Oxfam staff also worked with the men to persuade them of the value to the whole community of involving women in project activities and decision-making. Eventually, one by one, the men's and women's committees in the various centres decided to merge, and men and women heard the same things from the same Oxfam staff at the same time and were able to put their points of view with equal weight: the separate committees had served their purpose.

The role of Women's Co-ordinators

The development of women's representation was furthered by two female staff recruited specifically for this purpose. One of these was the daughter of the Kebkabiya Shertai who had been involved in representing women's views through the traditional authority structure; the other was recruited from the Social Development section of the EC-funded Jebel Marra Rural Development Project and had worked with *wadi* farmers. Their role would be to help the centres to form women's committees and to help to reflect the views of those committees at the PMC and to the technical staff.

The position of these Women's Co-ordinators in the team was problematic from the start. Having no technical skills or qualifications, they lacked credibility with both the village women and with the newer technical members of the team, who were themselves struggling with the transition from being technocratic experts in the Ministry of Agriculture to working for Oxfam as community development workers with a technical skill. Initial attempts to give the Women's Co-ordinators the training that they needed failed, and they became demoralised, reduced much of the time to working as Fur translators for the Arabic-speaking technical staff. In time, the Women's Coordinators became valued members of the team, but it was a painful first year for them. This illustrates the need for all members of a team to be committed to working for gender equity, and the need to train not only women's officers, but the team as a whole.

Addressing the particular concerns of women

The Women's Co-ordinators had also felt that the project should concentrate on the specific requests made by women for practical help with such things as poultry raising, food-processing, and traditional handicrafts. Previous attempts by Oxfam to deal with problems experienced by village women with regard to water-supply had been unsuccessful, as had a grinding mill, in both cases mainly for technical reasons.

The danger of concentrating on practical problems arising from women's workload and household responsibilities is that the fundamental inequalities which characterise women's place within society may go unrecognised and unchallenged. The distinction is often made between women's 'practical needs', and their more 'strategic needs', which involve changes in social attitudes (Moser, 1993). If women are viewed as a special group, with specific 'female' concerns that are only of peripheral concern to the main 'male' project, this can reinforce the very inequalities which the project is trying to address by emphasising women's subordinate position within specific areas of activity and interest, and formalising their exclusion from the main project.

In Kebkabiya, there was a feeling that introducing development initiatives specifically for women might encourage a belief that there is a 'natural' difference between a men's project, concerned with central issues of food security, and a women's project dealing with peripheral 'women's' interests. If the objectives of the women's project were to meet needs within the household, this might increase even further what has been termed the active 'domestication' of women (Rogers, 1980). In such a situation, the fundamental imbalance of power between funder and beneficiary community

Participation and gender

becomes evident; despite Oxfam's belief that participation in decision-making is vital for development, when local women stated their needs for support for their own income-generating activities, Oxfam's response was not entirely positive, because it was felt that such activities were unlikely to lead to genuine empowerment and development for the women.

A middle path

Many of the requests for funding being put forward by the village women were well thought out, and supporting the activities suggested might well contribute to building up the credibility of the project in their eyes. It was therefore agreed that the Project Coordinator would have a discretionary budget at his disposal with which to support those women's initiatives he viewed as complementary to the objectives of the project without losing sight of the priority aim of securing the full involvement of women in the core project activities.

Miriam Adam, one of the two Women's Coordinators and now Women's Officer with KSCS, acknowledges the role these small initiatives had played in getting women used to the idea that they had rights within the project and could make their voice heard:

> Not many income generation projects were approved in the first few years of this fund's operation. Those that were had to show that they met genuinely perceived needs, and that the women who proposed them were prepared to make direct demands themselves for project funds. In this way they had to get actively involved. It was a valuable learning process for them.

By 1992 it was felt that in a number of centres women were making sufficient use of the main project services to begin working systematically upon their other requests without jeopardising their increasing involvement in the main project. Miriam Adam comments:

> I now think that if we had implemented the separate women's income-generating activities earlier it would have led the women to believe that handicrafts projects and the like were all that Oxfam was prepared to offer them. But by this stage women had been sufficiently empowered by involvement in the main project to start using the voice they had gained to make additional demands regarding their other needs.

The role of women leaders

In some centres, active women's committees were established and women benefited much more directly from project activities. In others, however, women's involvement continued to be limited, especially in outlying villages.

Not surprisingly, perhaps, progress often depended upon the mould-breaking work of particular individuals. In Shoba centre, for example, women appear to have been much more directly involved at all stages. Shoba (together with Um Baldiso) was one of two new centres to be admitted to the project in 1989, at the start of Phase Two and at the request of the villagers themselves. Now an active member of KSCS's Executive Committee, Amouna Mohammed Hamid describes the process:

> ❝ The original idea to apply for inclusion in the Oxfam project came from the village teacher [a man who remains closely involved in the project and is himself a member of KSCS's Executive Committee] but the women were consulted about it before the letter of application was drafted.
>
> I am the daughter of the village Sheikh and so I have a familiarity with handling social issues and a knowledge of the Arabic language that other women may not have. Ebada [one of the Oxfam Women's Co-ordinators] came to the village to help us to set up the women's committee and we called a general meeting of the village women and chose a committee of six women which I was asked to lead.
>
> We then brought in the other villages in the centre to arrange the division of labour for the construction of a seedbank store in the village and we were able to ensure that the work was divided equitably: women collected sand for making the cement and the men collected mud with which to make the bricks.
>
> Later on, when literacy classes were started, I was one of the first students and I used them as an opportunity to discuss our general needs. I think that women in Shoba are different. I try to lead by example but the involvement of Shoba women in the project isn't down to me. We know that we have to stand up for our rights if we are to secure them. Although there's a fifty-fifty representation on the village sugar committee, for example, the male members still try to exclude the women from the actual distribution so that they can keep the extra amount allocated as a payment for doing this task for themselves. We're working on this problem! Women are also involved on the Shoba Village Council.

> There's a mixed project committee in the centre at which the women do speak up, but there are separate pre-meetings for women only in all the villages. I try to attend all of these to make sure that they are properly informed. I have been surprised to see how much more submissive the women in other project centres are. I would say to them that they need to watch the men all the time and make sure they know what's going on. If there are Landrovers in the village they need to find out what they are doing there. They can't expect to get their rights if they let the men take control. '

This fighting talk, backed by solid action, is, however, rare in the project area. It remains unclear whether Amouna is being falsely modest in claiming that she is not the instigator of the proactive approach of the women in this centre, or whether there really is something exceptional in the culture of the village that makes it different. Either way, what is clear is that the women of Shoba have benefited more than most from the project's activities as a result of their active participation in its decision-making structures.

In other villages, women have clearly been excluded from project benefits by men. In some cases, this appears to have been deliberate: for instance, while one centre sent a female representative to the PMC in accordance with Oxfam's request, the villages only sent male representatives to their VCC. Women in one village in this centre, where there has only been a female representative since the March 1994 committee re-elections, described their relationship with the project:

> ' It's better than nothing, but we haven't got much from the project. Before we selected Howa [the woman representative to the PMC], we had no way of asking for things from the project. We didn't even know what was on offer unless the men brought us things. The men in this village don't do much for the women. We've heard that in Dadi [another project centre], for instance, the people on the committee have got much more for the women there. Now that we have a representative of our own we should get to hear through her about what the project can do for us. '

Increasing the scope for involvement

Rogaya Yusif of Dadi centre, who later trained as a paravet, one of three women to do so, began to be involved with the project when she was selected by the women of her village to represent them to the VCC. Being the only literate female representative to the VCC she was then asked to be the centre's female representative to the PMC in Kebkabiya.

> Women's representation on the committees is very important. If the representative is concerned with women's development then there's a lot that can be done for women in the villages through the project. As well as the core services, Oxfam has helped us to deepen the well here, has arranged training for the local midwife, and laid on literacy and health education classes. It's not very likely that this would have happened without female representation on the committees.

Rogaya's husband agrees:

> Male representatives will try to tell people about the services the project is offering, but inevitably the men will get to hear about things first from them and often the female-headed households won't hear at all. Having female representatives is the only way of ensuring that women get to hear about what the project is doing.

Rogaya herself stood down from the committee when she was selected for training as the centre's paravet.

Under the guidance of Soad Mustafa, recruited as Oxfam Darfur's Women's Officer from the Range and Pasture Department of the Ministry of Agriculture, a number of new activities started. The first of these were income-generating activities such as food-processing, household market-gardening, poultry farming, and the establishment of co-operative shops and women's community farms. Soad stresses the role of these 'women-specific projects' in helping to realise the gender objectives of the broader project:

> These projects have helped women to feel closer to the organisation and at the same time have helped men to respect the involvement of women. The organisation of food processing activities, for instance, helped women get used to organising themselves into committees and work groups and also got them used to analysing their economic situation and the issues it raised for production and marketing. The men saw this and realised that there was a benefit to the whole community. In the case of some activities, such as literacy classes, they have even been requesting them for themselves. In other cases, men from villages where an activity was not happening have been pressing the project to run it with the women of their village.

In 1993 in a major joint initiative, Oxfam helped the VCCs each to select two village midwives for formal training in El Fasher. The thirty-two midwives were then given a two-month course of training at the Ministry of Health in El Fasher, funded by Oxfam, with UNICEF presenting them with a case of equipment to take away and use in their subsequent practice.

Women's literacy training

Another area of intervention was the establishment of women's literacy classes. If women were to increase in confidence and to become more involved over time in the direct management of the project, then the problem of their educational handicap had to be tackled and they had to be equipped with the basic skills necessary for the project's administration. Staff were also well aware of the potential of literacy education for raising social development issues that stretched well beyond women's immediate circumstances.

Although women's literacy had been first identified for a potential intervention several years previously, nothing had been done about it. But when a new literacy project was launched by Oxfam which happened to coincide with a similar initiative by the Ministry of Education, it became possible to pool resources. Oxfam provided finance to enable teachers from the area to go to El Fasher for training in literacy methods. Not surprisingly, there was considerable enthusiasm from the village women about the initiative; equally unsurprisingly, many of them dropped out during the course of tuition. However, by the end of the first year of the two-year course, 277 women were still attending regularly. (The drop-out rate of just over 30 per cent is one that many adult education teachers in developed countries would be proud to replicate.) The initiative has encouraged women to participate in other aspects of the project and increased demand for its services.

Because literacy cannot be effectively taught in a vacuum — people have to be taught to read and to write *about* something — it provides an excellent opportunity to stimulate people to question some of the factors affecting their lives (Freire, various dates). The Oxfam/KSCS approach has made great use of this dual nature of literacy education. The classes have helped women to reflect on and analyse their experience in new ways and, more practically, raise awareness of some of the things the project could do for them. The project's animal traction officer, for instance, reports that demand for ploughs from women is greatly enhanced in those villages where literacy classes have taken place.

Maintaining the momentum

The formal transfer of the project's management from Oxfam to the KSCS, which will be described in the next chapter, brought another attempt to ensure that women were fully represented. Many of the representatives of village women were elected in March 1994 when an election committee from Oxfam, KSCS and Ministry of Social Welfare staff toured the centres ensuring that the elections in each village were properly conducted.

Each VCC is now properly constituted to send its representatives to the PMC in Kebkabiya. Women in many villages reported a sense of a new beginning:

> Things should get better now. If anything comes to the store we should be told about it by our representative, Fatma. We've already had meetings to discuss the availability of ploughs and seeds for next rainy season. Before, we only got to hear that there were things available when the men came back from the centre with their allocations. By the time we got there it had often all been distributed. (Woman in Rai)

Shortly before the handover of the project to KSCS, Miriam Adam transferred from Oxfam to work as the Women's Officer at the Society. There, she continues the activities she inherited from Oxfam but additionally has recruited and trained ten female rural extension workers. Where possible these workers have been recruited from among the villagers themselves, and are mainly young literate women with a commitment to their villages. Where it has not been possible to recruit suitable women locally, secondary school graduates from Kebkabiya have been appointed. They conduct women's literacy and numeracy classes (which include the development of Arabic language skills) and promote community health and environmental protection. In addition, they work with the VEAs, paravets, and centre committees to ensure that women benefit fully from the core activities of the Society.

Should the pilot scheme prove a success, Miriam hopes for a further extension of this initiative to other villages in the project area in the very near future. Although the scheme had only been running a couple of months at the time of field work for this book, the attendance and level of participation in classes run by Hadia Hassan Adam at Debli, for example, indicate great initial enthusiasm. The community had put resources of its own into the scheme, with every participating household contributing LS100 and a bowl of grain towards Hadia's living expenses and the local Popular Committee agreeing to provide kerosene for the hurricane lamps used in the classes, which are mainly held after sunset when women have finished their domestic chores.

Soad Mustafa, Women's Officer appointed in 1992, points to some of the broader benefits of the women's extensionist scheme:

> The extensionists reduce the burden of work that the women-specific projects create for Miriam, freeing her to spend more time liaising with the other components of the project to ensure women's participation. They also enable her to concentrate her work in those villages where women still lag behind the others — for there are still great differences between the centres regarding women's participation.
>
> Once she has challenged the established order of things, the extensionists can then build upon her work. It's a long process and I very much hope that the handover period [from Oxfam to KSCS] will be long enough to allow for full coverage of the project area. Only this will ensure that women throughout the area have sufficient understanding of their position in the project to ensure that they remain fully involved without having to rely upon a few particularly strong individuals to stand up for them.

As far as the full participation of women in the project's structures and activities is concerned, the project has achieved much but there is a vast amount yet to do. Development of this aspect of the project's work is not only incomplete; it is also very uneven. In the words of one KSCS member, 'women are the gate-keepers of rural development.' Much work will be needed if the Kebkabiya project is going to open this particular gate on a permanent basis across its whole area.

Both Soad and Miriam point to increased coverage of the women's extensionist programme as a major activity to be consolidated over the coming years, and to the development of a revolving fund to provide credit for women's enterprises as the next stage in women's empowerment. As Soad puts it:

> the projects to date have decided collectively with women the activities they will get involved in; the credit fund will put the whole income-generating approach on a different basis by giving each individual woman the chance to develop ideas of her own.

Empowering communities

above Staff of KSCS in the office compound, Kebkabiya

Moving towards independence 5

In early 1990, at the height of its direct involvement in the project's management and implementation, Oxfam employed and managed all the technical and support staff required to implement project activities; ran and serviced all vehicles; purchased, distributed, and kept records of all inputs; and provided all the finance and financial management.

Oxfam also determined the overall strategy and policy of the project, ensuring consultation with the community and its most vulnerable members especially through its own commitment to anti-poverty strategies and community empowerment. It also ensured that the project's inter-agency liaison and public relations functions worked well enough to secure the support of government and other national and international bodies.

But this level of involvement could not continue indefinitely, and plans were already being made to hand over responsibility to the community. An evaluation of the Kebkabiya project carried out in 1992 pointed out that there was a considerable amount of work to be done by Oxfam before handover could be considered. The evaluation team recommended that Oxfam should maintain an operational input for at least a further four years, but that during this period the staffing of the Oxfam team should be scaled down and more emphasis should be placed upon imparting management skills and an understanding of the processes of community development to the KSCS membership. Over the next few months, the Kebkabiya team worked on a new strategic plan, drawing from and adapting the recommendations of the evaluation report. From now on, the Society began to think in terms of an interim period between Oxfam control and full community management, when project activities would be carried out by a paid staff body directly employed by the Society and replicating many of the functions of the Oxfam team.

To a large extent, the project had always been staffed by Sudanese. In its ten-year history the project had only had one expatriate manager, who was in post for just a year. In addition, three medium-term expatriate consultants have been employed by the project, living at Kebkabiya for periods of six months to a year at a time. Two of these, however, were specifically hired to develop local management frameworks and the third had a precisely defined technical brief in relation to animal traction work. From 1988 onwards the Project Co-ordinator has been a local member of Oxfam's staff, for the majority of that period, Salih Abdel Mageed.

While the Project Co-ordinator reported to a Regional Representative based in El Fasher who has, for more than seven years of the project's history, been an expatriate, there have been two spells when this post too has been in Sudanese hands. More significantly, during the lengthy period when the post was vacant between 1991 and 1993 the Kebkabiya team had been obliged to learn to become self-reliant in much the same way that KSCS was being asked to become. In many respects the handover would be from one local NGO to another.

An event or a process?

The crucial element of a successful handover must be sustainability. If handover consists of the process of transferring all activities from an outside organisation to a local structure, then it can only be said to have been completed when the new structure has a stable future that can adapt to all foreseeable circumstances at least as well as the original international NGO. In that sense, handover should not be seen as an event, but as a progress towards an eventual goal.

However, towards the end of 1992, changes in government policy made the future of foreign NGOs working in the country uncertain. Oxfam management in Khartoum and Oxford decided to impose a tight, one-year timetable in which to complete the handover, a decision which reflected the very real concerns felt by Oxfam about its future presence in Sudan. It was essential for contingency plans to be in place to ensure the viability of projects, particularly if Oxfam were to be unable to provide continuing operational support.

Such a strategy caused considerable consternation amongst the staff who had, hitherto, been working on the assumption that a handover would take place over a four-year period, with a further period of at least two years' direct support from Oxfam.

A negative reaction

The decision to go for an accelerated handover was largely perceived by Oxfam staff and KSCS members as Oxfam 'washing its hands' of the project. Staff felt they were being asked to work themselves out of jobs for which there was no obvious replacement in Darfur in terms of both remuneration and professional satisfaction. They had also invested considerable intellectual and emotional energy — over a period of seven years in some cases — into the creation of a development project that had attracted glowing reports from many different visitors: the Kebkabiya project is often seen as a model for rural community development in the Sudan. A handover that was carried out in a rush threatened to destroy everything they had achieved over the years.

Staff concerns were echoed unanimously by villagers. The project had brought material and social benefits that they valued greatly. However, while villagers had no difficulty with the objective of placing full managerial autonomy into the hands of the community, they were concerned that this should be done carefully and with adequate support and supervision over a long period:

> The idea [of the handover] is fine but is the timing right? Oxfam will have to stay with KSCS a long time until they are sure that the services will continue to the same standard. I have some concern that they won't be able to deliver services because they won't have the resources. It will take time to get the finances of the Society right.
> (Village sheikh and VCC member)

> The idea is OK but will require a lot of supervision. If things don't work out then Oxfam should be prepared to step in again until they get it right.
> (Female villager)

> The project has worked well under Oxfam because of the regular contact between Oxfam and the villagers. Will KSCS be able and willing to come to us as often? We don't mind paying a membership fee but will we get value for our money? (Female villager)

> KSCS can certainly take over the work of Oxfam, but you will need to give them a lot of support. If you let go of them too suddenly they'll collapse. Oxfam has to develop the Society's abilities just as the foreign staff of Oxfam have developed [individual] Sudanese abilities. (Male villager)

> The handover is a good idea in principle but I have real reservations. KSCS has to continue the work that Oxfam started and to the same standard. The people will be happy to pay a little extra to ensure that the services do continue, but if KSCS activities start to cost more than the market prices then the basic objectives will have changed. It's a fine balance that will have to be worked out carefully. (Village sheikh)

A more flexible approach to the handover

Because of such views, and its own misgivings about an accelerated handover, Oxfam accepted that such a timetable could only be justified if there were an imminent threat to the organisation's future in the country. With that apparent threat no longer on the horizon, Oxfam has reverted to the more developmental idea that handing over is a process, rather than an event.

The Society's Chairman, Omer Idris, however, still believes that the original timetable was the better one, but concedes that 'with the flexibility that has been shown and ongoing support I believe we can make the handover work in its current form'.

Community participation and specialist staff

Members of VCCs could fairly quickly acquire an understanding of many of the processes of administrative control, and they were offered training on an informal basis from the earliest stages of the project, with Oxfam staff using actual examples from the project as training material. However, financial book-keeping was a different matter. In 1992 the Regional Accountant in the El Fasher office — Farrah Omer Bello — was transferred to the project to strengthen its administrative systems. In order to ensure a satisfactory level of record-keeping, however, he found it necessary to move much of the administrative control back to Kebkabiya.

Once systems had been established which could give an accurate picture at any time of the payments to, receipts from, and outstanding loans owed by each of the sixteen centres, control had to be passed back to the PMC. Reluctant to put such complex records back into the hands of the VCCs, the PMC decided that, by virtue of the KSCS Treasurer's background in accountancy, he should take full control of the funds himself.

The problem was, however, that as the only qualified accountant within the communities served by the project, he was irreplaceable as a PMC member. Furthermore, there was a problem of control and potential conflict of interest in putting so much responsibility in the hands of one member of the PMC. It was therefore decided that he should resign from the Committee and be employed as a salaried member of the KSCS staff. This put him under the direct management control of the PMC and created a budget which will enable his replacement by another qualified accountant when he eventually leaves the project.

The appointment of an accountant was the first step in the creation of a professional staffing structure under community control, as an alternative to handing over the project activities directly to the community. The PMC felt that leaving the majority of tasks in the hands of community-based committees and extension workers, as envisaged back in 1988, was not yet feasible. As one PMC member explains:

> ❦ We gave a lot of thought to this matter but felt that the VCCs, VEAs and paravets had not yet acquired the necessary level of administrative and technical competence to operate without professional support. We will always need some permanent staff presence in Kebkabiya as the committee members live in their own outlying communities, but we accept that the current structure is a temporary arrangement.
>
> We intend to decrease the staff size and financial outlay over the next few years, but this will depend upon increasing the strength of the democratic structure as the Society's members gain in their understanding of it. At the moment all staff are employed on one-year contracts, which gives us managerial flexibility and also gives them an incentive to perform well in order to secure the renewal of their contracts for the following year. ❦

The PMC decided to seek funding for the creation of new posts for a Veterinary Officer, Agricultural Officer, Women's Officer, Secretary, and two drivers in the 1993–4 budget. Consideration had also been given to relying upon technical support from Ministry of Agriculture staff in Kebkabiya but the idea was rejected for reasons that Omer Idris, Chair of the PMC, explains:

> ❦ There is a high turnover among Government staff and posts are often vacant for lengthy periods. This would disrupt developmental continuity and mean that these staff would rarely have the opportunity to gain the necessary familiarity with the project's objectives and ways of working. More important, as Government officials they would have their own reporting structure and so could not be brought under the democratic control of the Society's committees. ❦

The new staffing structure

The new staffing structure of the KSCS virtually replicates that used by Oxfam when the project was operational. The KSCS has an Executive Director who manages the staff on a day-to-day basis, reporting to the Chair of the Management Committee. The senior operational staff — an Agricultural Officer, a Livestock Officer and a Women's Officer — each head up their project components, and in addition a Veterinary Officer was appointed to manage a new project component. The Agricultural and Women's Officers have transferred directly from Oxfam to the Society, whilst the Animal Traction Officer remains on secondment from ITDG. The Animal Traction component has yet to be handed over, but when it is, the ATO will report to the Agricultural Officer rather than heading up a stand-alone component.

Omer Idris is clear that the creation of this professional staff body was a direct result of the possible need for the Society to take up the reins from Oxfam far more quickly than had been anticipated in the original project design:

> *KSCS would look very different now if the recommendations of the evaluation had been accepted, primarily because by the time that handover occurred the beneficiaries and the VCCs would have been much better equipped to carry out the job without professional support. What you now see is a direct result of the accelerated handover.*

The practicalities of a handover

The processes of handover for the Kebkabiya project may be considered under three broad headings: operational handover; management handover; and financial handover. At the time of writing, the first of these is almost completed, the second is in progress, and the third has for the most part yet to begin. Once the debate about the timetable had been resolved, *operational handover* proceeded largely on a component-by-component basis.

Operational handover

Agriculture
The first element of the project to be handed over was the agricultural component. The relative ease with which this took place was a product of two factors: the fairly early stage of development of its activities, and the presence of a suitable candidate for the post of Agricultural Officer.

The agricultural component has had a somewhat chequered history, being formed out of the merger of two original initiatives: agricultural extension and pest control. The intention had been to focus on non-chemical methods of pest control, but post-holders had received little support in developing sustainable and 'low-tech' interventions. Part of this problem stemmed from the fact that their own training and experience had been largely focused on the use of chemical and other technical inputs that would be difficult to transfer to community control.

At the time of the creation of the KSCS, the Society was fortunate to have available to it the services of a graduate agriculturalist with personal reasons for settling in the Kebkabiya area and a deep commitment to treating agricultural extension as a branch of community development. His appointment to the Society, originally as an voluntary worker, brought a new community-based approach; and when he took over as the Society's Agricultural Development Officer he was left to develop those activities with which he had already been most closely involved and which were closest to the spirit of the original project objectives: VEA training and the management of a revolving credit fund. At the request of the PMC he cut back on the more technically demanding activities instigated by his predecessors, thereby bringing the component's activities much more directly under the control of the community representatives on the committee.

The women's component

The operational handover of the project's initiatives with women was achieved in tragic circumstances. The Oxfam team on this component consisted of three people. These were the two original Fur-speaking Women's Co-ordinators recruited at the commencement of the project's second phase in 1989, and their supervisor, Oxfam's Regional Women's Officer, Soad Mustafa.

The original idea had been that one of the two Fur-speakers, Ebada Abdel Gabbar, would transfer to the Society as its Women's Officer with the other, Miriam, taking on the animal traction component under the supervision of the Agricultural Development Officer. However, in June 1993, Ebada was killed when the lorry in which she was travelling on leave to her home village of Nyertete was ambushed by bandits.

Despite this setback, the women's component has now been handed over to be managed by KSCS. Soad emphasises that there is a lot to be done before Oxfam can regard it as free-standing under its new management:

> ❛ You have to remember that this component was started after all the others and will therefore probably continue to require support after them. The KSCS committee members do increasingly understand the core role of the [women's] component and that without a gender commitment there can be no sustainable development. However, the broader membership of the Society still needs working upon. The women-specific projects are the gateway to further development and change. Even when and if Oxfam eventually withdraws support from KSCS it should continue to fund these activities separately because the continuing presence of Oxfam behind this component is the surest guarantee that it will continue to be given priority. ❜

In January 1995, three co-operative shops were opened, with some 40 women taking advantage of the credit schemes on offer through the KSCS. To mitigate against the effects of inflation, the credit was not in cash but in kind, for example, equipment and a bulk supply of tea that allows a woman to set up as a tea seller in her village or in her local market. The choice of who should get the benefit of such facilities was made by village centre committees.

In March 1995, a workshop for women was held by the KSCS for women and men extension workers, members of project management committees, and invited representatives from government departments. In all, 46 women and men took part in the workshop, which covered a number of topics including participation, empowerment, and the planning and monitoring of projects, all of which were addressed from the perspective of heightening gender awareness within KSCS project areas. However, in spite of the success of the credit schemes and the workshop, the numbers of women signing on for literacy classes during the same period declined. The reasons given by women were the usual ones of lack of time and too many jobs to do both inside and outside the household.

Animal health

The livestock component was always going to require its own professional staff, because under Sudanese law, veterinary drugs may only be dispensed under the supervision of a qualified veterinarian. The question that remained, however, was that of continuing resource mobilisation and this was resolved by the establishment of a community veterinary pharmacy within the KSCS office complex. The pharmacy was formally opened during October 1994 and now serves members of the community — who may bring their animals for diagnosis and purchase drugs over the counter — and paravets from the project centres who have a credit allowance of drugs that they may draw from the pharmacy.

Oxfam's Veterinary Officer remained at the project during the induction of the KSCS vet, before returning to El Fasher. He will continue to make periodic visits to provide support and to ensure the smooth running of the pharmacy while it works itself up to full capacity. With this supervision, the component is now virtually handed over to the KSCS and seems likely to be the only component that can not only finance itself, but also return a small operating profit to the Society as a contribution towards the overhead expenses incurred in servicing it. As previously discussed, it also seems likely to remain the only component to be able to do this in the foreseeable future.

Animal traction

The final component, animal traction, had not begun its handover process at the time of writing, though the recruitment of a counterpart to the ITDG agricultural engineer should now be under way. Animal traction will be subsumed into the agricultural component, and once the final modifications to the implements have been made, it should not longer be necessary to employ a qualified agricultural engineer.

However, before that point is reached, some problems have to be resolved. The main implement delivered by the project is the all-steel plough and supply is likely to become more and more problematic because the raw steel required for its manufacture is becoming increasingly scarce and expensive.

Project staff have been experimenting with a mainly wooden design based on the Ethiopian *ard*, which uses steel only for the plough-share itself. Final modifications to the *ard* need to made and then the blacksmiths have to be trained in its manufacture and farmers persuaded that it is not a second-best implement. At present it is widely felt to be not robust enough for the Kebkabiya soils.

In order to facilitate raw material distribution and plough production it is currently proposed to establish a central blacksmiths' workshop in Kebkabiya. Until recently it was being conceived of as an income-generating venture which would bear the costs of the component much as the pharmacy is projected to bear the marginal costs of the veterinary component. This misunderstanding of the core role of the workshop probably arose out of the confusion generated by the proposal for an accelerated handover and the lack of clarity at that time as to what handover actually involved.

However, once it was agreed that the aim of self-sustainability was inappropriate and possibly incompatible with the main objective, to improve agricultural production, the establishment of the workshop as a blacksmiths' co-operative could go ahead. Blacksmith's groups are expanding, with successful workshops being held to upgrade new member's skills and thus ensure a sustainable supply of ploughs and other agricultural equipment. In spite of the price of raw steel doubling in the year 1994-95, 255 donkey ploughs have now been manufactured. The rise in steel prices was partially offset by taking a loan out from the central revolving fund, which meant that the metal could be purchased in bulk.

Other considerations

Certain operations will remain difficult for KSCS to carry out on its own for the simple reason that they take place in El Fasher or even Khartoum. These are, primarily, purchasing and forwarding, and the maintenance of vehicles.

Some purchases will have to be supervised by professional staff. Veterinary drugs, in particular cannot, by law, be purchased in Sudan unless there is a veterinary doctor in supervision. It would seem an unjustifiable sacrifice of scarce resources to the principle of independence to have the Society's vet travel to Khartoum for every purchase when Oxfam's own Livestock Officer, based in Khartoum, could provide invaluable support to the Society by fulfilling this task on their behalf (as he already does for other projects in Juba, Renk and Tokar elsewhere in Sudan).

For Oxfam, as well as for a local NGO, the maintenance of vehicles in a fieldworthy state has been a constant preoccupation over the years. In order to minimise difficulties, KSCS has built up a transport fleet that mixes locally purchased petrol-engined Landrover 109 vehicles with others from the more powerful and recent 110 range that have been donated by Oxfam. The KSCS has also employed its own Kebkabiya-based mechanic, a former Oxfam employee, and has a contract with the Save the Children workshop in El Fasher for major services.

Handing over management responsibilities

The creation of the PMC at the beginning of Phase Two and its formalisation in the registration and constitution of KSCS provided a structure which would eventually be able to carry out the *management* of the project. The next challenge was to ensure that the PMC had sufficient understanding of the tasks that it would be required to take on as a manager. As discussed above, while committee members had shown considerable vision in planning and policy formation for the project, the administrative skills of running a large and complex project had proved harder to pass on and this had resulted in decisions to employ professional staff to carry out specialised tasks. Nevertheless, in order to hold these staff accountable to the democratic structure of the Society, the elected members would need sufficient knowledge of the tasks involved to supervise their employees.

Throughout the second phase of the project, Oxfam staff had placed renewed emphasis on passing on management skills and ensuring familiarity with the basic processes of project administration and resource mobilisation. From 1992 onwards, a more formal training programme was introduced. Three week-long courses in different aspects of social and community development have been held for committee members, taught by Oxfam and KSCS staff and colleagues from the Ministries of Agriculture and Social Welfare; and two courses of two weeks each, taught by staff of the Al Fanar management development centre in Khartoum. These courses have concentrated upon 'hard' management skills, such as administrative procedures, financial management and accounting, the management of people, and project logistics and input distribution. Even PMC members with a low level of literacy who have attended these courses have said that they found them valuable. In addition, the Chair and other honorary officers of the Society have attended specific training events and seminars, including an Oxfam course for African partners in Project Planning and Management held in Zambia.

An immediate problem arises from the fact that the democratic principles on which the KSCS is based mean that there is likely to be a high turnover of trained PMC members. A number of the people who had attended the courses mentioned above lost their PMC seats in the elections of March 1994. Although in itself this should be welcomed as a sign that its democratic systems are working well, the Society does, however, face the loss of training inputs to former committee members. However, potential candidates who have not had such training should not thereby be disadvantaged in standing against incumbent committee members. Both these factors point to committee training as a constant requirement for the Society, which will have to regard training as a cyclical process. A rolling programme of training in development and management skills will have to become one of its core activities.

Committee members will also need management information as well as skills in order to be able to carry out their role, and this points to the need for an effective monitoring system. This is something that the project has never really had. A system was established in early 1990 to monitor project activities and developments, but this was designed to serve the needs for management information of a largely graduate team at the project and of a mainly European line of management in El Fasher, Khartoum, and Oxford. Their information needs are very different from those of elected members based in the actual community that is being monitored.

Current PMC members vary widely in their assessment of whether or not they receive sufficient information to make good management decisions. Some feel that they do, though most accept that there are many things about the project that they do not fully understand. Several PMC members suggested that their duties only went so far as representing the interests of their own centre and that they had elected an Executive Committee to make policy decisions. This betrays a lack of understanding of the constitutional relationship between the two committees, but even members of the Executive Committee themselves accept that they do not always have a full grasp of the details. A PMC member from one of the remoter centres probably hit the nail on the head in commenting that:

> ❛ I know what I'm told about the project's activities but I have no way of knowing if there are other things that I ought to know. ❜

What is needed is a standardised set of indicators as management information, so that committee members are not reliant upon the variable content of unstructured staff reports. The Executive Committee are working on a more sophisticated set of performance indicators based on collation of information available from the representatives of the various centres. Combined with planned monthly workshops at which the Executive Committee will be able to question staff in detail about their activities, this should go a long way towards filling the current management information shortfalls.

As well as ensuring that the necessary hard management skills are in place, Oxfam has also been concerned that the commitment of committee members to policies compatible with its own is sufficient to enable its offspring to leave the organisational home without being promptly disinherited. Commitment to full community participation, a poverty focus, and gender sensitivity are enshrined in the KSCS constitution, but words need to be seen to be being translated into action.

Full management handover will also be dependent upon the Society learning to do without advice from Oxfam staff on some of the finer management skills such as personnel relations and the handling of organisational politics. Public relations might also be thought to come into this category, but the very high reputation of the Society and the exceptional esteem in which its work is held by politicians and government officials alike demonstrate that any special efforts in this direction are unnecessary. Indeed, it seems likely that amid the efforts of the present government to restore the sense of national pride of the Sudanese people, KSCS is more of a PR asset to Oxfam than *vice versa*. Oxfam will, however, have an ongoing role to play in supporting the Society in this field through its presence and contacts in El Fasher and Khartoum.

Personnel and organisational skills are difficult to teach and can really only be learned through experience. At present, staff seconded from Oxfam, in particular Farrah Omer Bello as the acting Chief Executive of the Society, have a key role to play in advising the Chair of the PMC and his colleagues on the handling of disputes and other contentious issues. To quote Meadows (1994) again:

> A poor personnel decision resulting in a complaint laid with the local authorities could put the KSCS at serious risk, where an Oxfam employee would be more likely to follow an internal complaints procedure.

Moving towards independence

Although the Society is becoming adept at the management of internal disputes within the committees, the main area in which its skills in organisational politics will have to be developed is that of staff relations. If the experience of other organisations (up to and including national governments) is anything to go by, there is a greater danger of genuine democratic control and accountability being lost to a small elite of paid officials than to any internal faction within the community.

One of the main building blocks in the development of the KSCS as an institution — the appointment of a Chief Executive — has yet to be put in place and the trepidation with which the Executive Committee are facing this task clearly reveals their unease about the potential ramifications. At the time of writing, the postponement of this step, by means of an extension of Farrah Omer Bello's secondment, is under careful consideration. It may well be that another year or so of management consolidation with the support of a trusted person with few vested interests in the directions of the Society's development will greatly enhance the eventual chances of success from this major appointment. Crucially, it may help the Society's committees to formulate a clearer idea of what are to be their eventual staffing requirements: it would be during the handover of activities from paid staff to committees that the interests of the two bodies would become most clearly divergent and the role of the Chief Executive would be most critical. Through whatever channels they may be delivered, Oxfam's services as an honest broker are likely to be highly valuable to the Society at this time.

Financial handover

The final and most difficult part of a complete handover is likely to be the *financial handover* of the project. Although many ideas about this are currently being revolved, there is no clear sense as to how financial independence may be achieved. The Society's annual budget is of the order of LS 25.5 million (£39,500 approx). To date, only three ways in which the Society may make a further contribution towards this amount have been identified:

- Reduce the overall amount required through the eventual reduction of the staffing establishment. This is intrinsically a valuable objective, though care will need to be taken to ensure that staff are not made redundant before their role has been fully taken over by the committee.

- Increase the level of subscriptions paid by the membership, currently at the rate of LS20 per month (less than half the cost of a glass of tea). The principle that some payment towards the services of the Society should be made by the membership is an important one, as it not only serves to consolidate a sense of ownership but also emphasise the members' *rights* to accountability. However, the PMC will have to resist any temptation to raise extra finance in future by increasing the membership fees to levels at which they would begin to become prohibitive to the poorest members of the community — the primary targets of Oxfam's and KSCS's mandate.

- Replicate the profit made by the community veterinary pharmacy in other project activities. Current projections are that the pharmacy should make a profit of LS6m (£9317 approx) per annum once it is working at full capacity. While this would enable the veterinary component to become self-financing (at least in terms of its marginal costs), it should nevertheless be treated with extreme caution as a model for other components. Quite simply, it does not seem possible within the current climate of high inflation that the sale of seasonal inputs — which are not as obviously a direct financial investment as the purchase of drugs to save the life of a valuable animal — can be made into a profitable venture.

Even if all of these three measures could be implemented with maximum effectiveness it seems unlikely that they would enable the Society to secure more than about 30 per cent of its funding from its own activities.

Any consideration of a way through this apparent impasse needs to address some fairly fundamental issues. The search for market-based solutions to questions of social policy world-wide has always failed where provision of services to the poorest is concerned. The poor, by definition, do not have at their disposal the resources that can convert their perceived and very real needs into effective market demand for the goods and services that would address those needs.

If external funding is not available then there are only two ways forward for the organisations that deliver services to poor people. The first is to compromise the principle of equal access by charging for services. This means either the effective withdrawal of services from the poorest or the introduction of some kind of means-testing to determine eligibility for subsidies. This in turn is costly and labour-intensive and all too often has the effect of acting as a barrier to those who most need the subsidies.

The second way forward is for service organisations to set up their own entirely separate fundraising activities to finance their operational work. It is solely in this way that Oxfam has been able to fund the Kebkabiya project hitherto. Oxfam obtains much of its income directly from the British public in a wide variety of ways; it is thus relatively independent from sources of funding such as grants from government and the European Union and has therefore a high degree of policy independence.

Although such a fundraising operation is obviously most likely to be successful in a rich country like the UK, where average disposable incomes enable a majority of people to contribute to charities if they so choose, there is undoubtedly considerable disposable personal wealth within poor countries (concentrated, admittedly, in fewer hands) and there are many examples of successful fundraising operations for charitable purposes in developing countries. The better established members of the HelpAge International family such as HelpAge India, HelpAge Kenya, and Pro Vida Columbia are examples that come to mind (Tout 1989). It may be the case that in the future KSCS will be able to develop a similarly successful programme of fundraising and that Oxfam, as an acknowledged market leader in the field of charitable fundraising, will have a major consultancy input to make at that time.

This third phase of the handover is, however, something for the future. The Society's committees have a major challenge on their hands in securing the sustainable functioning of the project's operational activities, establishing full management control over them, and consolidating the democratic management structure so that its foundations lie deep in the communities of Kebkabiya rather than superficially resting upon their more firmly established structures. A major effort towards financial independence at the present time would most likely prove, at best, a distraction from these tasks and at worst could end up by compromising them.

Empowering communities

above harvest time, near Kebkabiya

Towards the future 6

The process of erecting a tent begins by the fabric being stretched out on the ground, and then someone holds the supporting poles up to define the eventual shape. At this point the tent bears a superficial resemblance to the finished article; it is, however, entirely dependent upon the support provided by the person holding up the poles. Should this person let go of them at this stage then the whole structure will collapse. The hard work of securing the ropes by hammering in the ground pegs, to give the tent the ability to stand on its own and weather a storm, has still to be done. This is the stage of development which the KSCS has currently attained. The creation of a democratic structure and of a service delivery mechanism managed through that structure is a very considerable achievement, but it is still largely dependent upon support from Oxfam, its own staff, and the dedication and vision of a small number of its own members. There has been considerable progress towards a sense of community ownership of Society; and the constitution itself is a partial guarantee of the basic objectives. If an alternative source of finance could be found, the Society could probably survive the enforced withdrawal of Oxfam, though it is unlikely that this could be accomplished without some fairly drastic changes to its real nature and workings.

What can we learn from this account of the process of building community participation with a view to handing over an operational project to its beneficiaries? What are the factors which contribute towards a successful handover, and what are the problems that may be faced in the future? No major operational programme had ever been handed over by Oxfam to a community-based organisation before, and there were no models to be followed. But the Kebkabiya experience can provide useful lessons for other operational projects where the possibility of community management is being considered for the future. It is also a powerful illustration of the process of empowerment of the community, built on increasing participation of men and women in development activities, and the gradual assumption of responsibility for those activities.

Laying the foundations for independence

Oxfam, and many other development NGOs, have usually sought to fund local organisations to implement development initiatives they wished to support. It was because there were no suitable local partners with whom Oxfam could work that it had become operational on such a large scale in Kebkabiya. But the eventual necessity of some kind of handover to the community, and the form this might take, had been considered when the second phase of the project had been planned.

When the range of activities expanded in this second phase, it was in response to needs expressed by the communities themselves. The principle of consultation, of working with people to determine their needs and how best to respond to them, was fundamental to Oxfam's approach. When staff failed to observe these principles, as when extension agents were placed in five villages to organise farmer cooperatives, without first consulting the community, the resulting failure served to illustrate the importance of the principles.

So, from the start, Oxfam's approach had been to involve the community. People were consulted, were involved in implementation, were expected to manage aspects of the project. In this way, a sense of ownership was fostered from the outset. The first community management structures, the seedbank committees, established an understanding of the processes of community development, but were essentially similar to traditional village structures, in that they consisted almost exclusively of men, either self-appointed or nominated by traditional authorities in the villages. The later village committees created a new model of democratic community representation. Through them a sense of community responsibility could be fostered and managerial capacity developed.

A major consideration for Oxfam was how it could relinquish control without sacrificing the social gains for which it had struggled, especially in the field of gender relations. When the KSCS was formed, a step taken in preparation for the future handover of the project, the constitution drawn up for the new organisation enshrined the basic principles of democracy and gender equity which were the cornerstones of Oxfam's approach.

The management of a complex, multi-faceted development initiative requires experience and training. The need to provide training in management skills for members of the PMC was fully recognised by Oxfam. The intermediate stage of employing staff to carry out particular technical functions may be more or less prolonged, as discussed earlier. But even to manage staff requires a certain level of understanding of the functions they perform, so training for PMC members will remain an important activity for the foreseeable future.

Questions of sustainability

When an organisation which has previously been a dependent element in a larger organisation becomes independent, questions of sustainability are bound to arise. Sustainability has many aspects. There is basic organisational sustainability: the ability of an organisation to continue to function efficiently, to take sensible decisions and implement policies, to manage its assets and resources wisely, to set objectives and measure their attainment, to maintain its structures and yet be flexible in responding to changing circumstances. There is also a more intangible sustainability, in the preservation of essential principles and approaches. Independence is often equated with financial sustainability; for true independence, an organisation should be financially self-sustaining, not dependent on others for funds to maintain it. We will look at these different aspects of sustainability, and the problems which the KSCS may face in the future as it moves towards fuller independence.

Organisational sustainability

The discussions concerning the appointment of a Chief Executive have clearly revealed the fragility of the Society's structure. Whether it comes sooner or later, the handover of this key post from an Oxfam secondee and a trusted friend to a person specifically chosen for their managerial acumen and political dexterity will be a major test of the strength of the PMC and the Executive Committee. This will be particularly so if there are divergences of vision about the future directions of the Society — as there are bound to be at times.

The debates highlight another feature of the Society's current fledgling status, that of the dependency upon particular individuals. This is perhaps a stage in the development of any new venture or initiative, but sooner or later all the founding figures will move on. As long as there is a feeling that any or all of them are indispensable or irreplaceable, then the Society remains vulnerable and dependent. The Society's Chair, Omer Idris, for example, has headed the community's representative structure since the creation of the PMC in 1989. He now carries out a virtual full-time job for which he is only paid the actual expenses that he incurs in the course of his duties. The role leaves him with just enough time for the duties of his paid job as Kamonga's community health worker but not always enough for his own farming activities. How would the Society cope with his departure for paid employment? Would it find another Chair willing to invest such a huge amount of personal time and energy in the project? Would it need to?

There are others who at present would appear to be so closely identified with the development of their part of the project that they would seem difficult to replace. The departure in the immediate future of the Women's Officer would probably necessitate some serious organisational thought about the future development of gender equity within the project. Similarly, although agriculturalists are easier to recruit than women's development workers, the distinctive community-orientated approach of the Agricultural Officer to his part of the project is not a common attitude of mind. Until the project feels confident that it can recruit and induct replacements for key members such as these, and cope during their induction period before they become fully operational, then there will be a need for Oxfam to stand in readiness to catch hold of one the tent-poles if so required and requested.

Preservation of Oxfam principles and approach

The constitution drawn up when KSCS was created makes provision for procedures and approaches which, if followed, would ensure that the new organisation adhered to the same principles as those of the original manager of the Kebkabiya project. Anxieties have been expressed about two principles in particular: the commitment to representative democracy, and to gender equity. Are these merely paper promises, or have they been fully accepted by the members of KSCS? If KSCS is to remain an Oxfam project partner, and receive funding support, then it will have to demonstrate a level of commitment to these principles.

Democracy and accountability

In avoiding unrealistically utopian expectations, it is easy to become unnecessarily cynical. Some fears expressed early in the handover about the fact that a small number of people were coming to wield a lot of influence were probably unduly cynical. In a representative structure that seeks to give a voice to 11,000 households it is inevitable that natural leaders will emerge, and the system would be quite unworkable otherwise. The real questions that need to be asked are whether the disproportionate amount of power that these people acquire is legitimately gained, and whether they can be held accountable by their constituency.

At present there seems to be no reason to answer either of these questions in the negative. The great majority of villagers appear to know who their village representatives are and confirm that they had a say in their appointment. Elections to higher-level committees and posts have been supervised by Oxfam and KSCS staff and members of the Ministry of Social Welfare's El Fasher office, and the processes have been considered satisfactory. As an ongoing funder of the Society, Oxfam will no doubt seek observer status at future rounds of representative re-election.

Although there are biases in representation, and ways of minimising these will have to be kept under consideration, it seems quite acceptable for the Executive Committee to include one teacher, one health worker, and the daughter of a Sheikh, given that all three are from the communities they represent, and farm and keep animals themselves. The rise of any meritocracy that did *not* have such community roots would, however, be a warning sign. Less easy to guard against is the inevitable tendency for representatives from the centres closer to Kebkabiya to dominate the Executive Committee to the exclusion of those around the Jebel Marra and the Jebel Si in particular.

The relative disenfranchisement of those members who do not speak, read or write Arabic is another cause for concern, especially as such people are predominantly women. The price of democracy, here as elsewhere in the world, is likely to be eternal vigilance. The prerequisite for this vigilance, on the part of the whole community, will be an understanding of the value of what is to be defended. Eisa Adam, an Executive Committee member from the Kireiker centre, reflects the balance of realism and idealism that is likely to be required in stating the biggest problem for the Society over the next few years, and the one that most needs to be addressed:

> ❝ Raising the awareness of people about how KSCS works will be the real challenge. At present it's very low, at times non-existent. If people and committees are fully committed to the constitution then the Society should develop well. There's a need for extensive training of the whole KSCS membership so that the beneficiaries really know the objectives and procedures of the Society. ❞

Gender equity

Can the commitment to gender equity, which is a major criterion for Oxfam funding, survive the transition to community management? On the surface it would appear that the project has probably gone past the point of no return on this issue. The commitment to gender equity is unambiguously written into the KSCS constitution, both in terms of the Society's core objectives and of the levels of female representation on decision-making bodies: 50 per cent on the PMC and not less than 40 per cent on the Executive Committee.

This paper commitment seems to be backed up by real progress towards increased awareness of gender issues within the community. Many of the women said that they felt things had improved during the life of the project:

> ❝ In the early years of the project the men would go down to Debli to collect the inputs and then they would decide between them who got what. Now women have a similar level of participation in the project. We get the same information and we are all involved in the collection and distribution of goods. Things are much improved for women. ❞
> (Woman in Sortani)

What is at least as important is that the attitudes of men seem to be changing. Those interviewed during the research for this book not only unanimously welcomed the inclusion of women in the project's decision-making structures as well as its actual service delivery activities, but were able to give convincing reasons why they believed this to be a positive development:

> Women are involved in agriculture just as much as the men so if we are trying to improve food production in the village we can only help on all the farms if we involve the women as well as the men. (Man in Bora)

> The village has many needs and the men can only be expected to know about a certain number of these. Women have their own specific concerns and their involvement on the committees has brought benefits to us that the men would never have thought to ask about. (Man in Somati)

There does, however, remain cause for concern. Many of the village women still feel that they are not fully benefiting from the project or have only begun to do so. It was apparent that women have in general received fewer benefits from the project and have less understanding of its workings. One women's representative said that while things had improved there were still problems:

> We were very angry about not receiving services, despite the fact that they had been promised to us, in the early years of the project, but things are much improved now. We've received seeds, ploughs and veterinary treatment for our animals but there can still be problems. For instance, last year the amount of pesticide that was delivered was not sufficient for our needs. The men ended up getting virtually all of it, not because there was a deliberate policy of exclusion but because they were able to go round to the VEA's house and to put pressure on him to come to their fields the following day. Women can't exert the same pressure so although he said that he would come to our fields he ended up going to those of the men who were leaning on him the hardest.

The same woman made the interesting point that while the (male) VEA in the village has been provided with a donkey for his work, she has to go to Kebkabiya on foot — a journey which takes six hours. She clearly felt that this indicated a under-valuing of women's representation; it prevented her from going around the villages to gather views and disseminate project information.

The most spectacular (though not the greatest) gains for women remain those delivered by projects aimed specifically at them rather than through the core workings of the main food-security activities. However, the involvement of women should not become 'a series of (admittedly very effective and empowering) Women Specific Projects regarded as a sideshow compared with the 'important' agricultural interventions' (Meadows, 1994).

There remains a long way to go before gender equity is a reality rather than a target and the danger for the project probably lies more in the direction of complacency than of hostility. Staff and members of the Management and Executive Committees need to remain mindful that the very real achievements of the Society to date are only a beginning and are probably quite fragile; there is much work to do before the gender-related objectives of the Society are irrevocably entrenched in the collective consciousness of the project's beneficiaries, male and female.

Financial sustainability

In the previous chapter, we referred to the difficult balance that had to be maintained between raising significant income from membership fees and by charging for services, and keeping those user-costs low enough not to act as a barrier excluding poor people from the befits of the project. These issues lie at the heart of much social policy debate in the rich countries at the present time and it is unrealistic to believe that they could be resolved by the KSCS when they are proving so intractable to politicians and academics in Europe, Australia and northern America.

Because it is clear that the Society is a long way from being able to finance its own activities, Oxfam has committed itself to funding the Society for at least a further five years. While this gives the Society a reasonable breathing space, both organisations need to be clear about what is to be accomplished during this period. There are perhaps lessons to be drawn here from the development in recent years of the so-called 'contract culture' within the UK voluntary sector (Adirondack and Macfarlane, 1992). This describes the trend away from vague and non-specific funding arrangements between voluntary organisations and (mainly) local government funders towards a more precisely agreed set of service-purchasing arrangements written into a service agreement or, less commonly, a legally binding contract. While such agreements have to be carefully negotiated on both sides, the advantage to the funder is that the nature of the service they are purchasing for their target beneficiaries is defined; the advantage to the service provider is that they have security of funding for the period of the agreement and a statement of what they must do during that period in order to maximise the chances of getting the arrangement renewed.

Such an agreement between Oxfam and the KSCS could be valuable in specifying the steps towards eventual independence that might be taken over the next five years. It would clarify the various phases of the Kebkabiya project.

If the first phase was about getting to know the community, the second about the establishment of service delivery mechanisms, and the third about the establishment of the KSCS, then the fourth would be about management capacity-building and the consolidation of accountability to the community. Although there are management skills that can usefully be developed during the next five years, such as budget preparation and grant application presentations, it is only in the fifth phase that the KSCS would start moving in earnest towards financial autonomy.

At that stage there will be a number of options to be considered to bridge the gap between the annual budgetary requirements of the Society (which should by then be much more settled than they are at present) and the income that can be earned from revolving funds and membership subscriptions, without compromising the basic objectives. The establishment of carefully planned fundraising activities, carried out by *ad hoc* PMC sub-committees or by staff employed specifically for the purpose, will be one option. The other will be the search for a sustainable source of grant income. Oxfam will need to be clear in its own mind what its position is towards the long-term grant-aiding of a partner organisation. Why should it *not* continue making core-cost grants to the Society for the foreseeable future? Would this be acceptable to its own donors, for the most part British taxpayers used to providing long-term funding to public services either directly or indirectly through their taxes and often to providing long-term assistance through covenants and other mechanisms to voluntary organisations working in the UK?

Another option would be for the Society to be actively encouraged to seek other sources of Northern funding. A successful approach to, for instance, the Save the Children Fund would, on the one hand, enhance its independence from its original funder and creator; on the other hand it would mean taking on a new set of reporting and monitoring requirements without any qualitative advance in sustainable self-sufficiency. It may, however, be that the long-term political direction of the Sudan is towards closer ties with the Arab and Islamic world and away from the West. In this case the Society might feel more secure by broadening its portfolio of funders to include support from perhaps the Red Crescent societies of Islamic countries or indeed from in-country funders if these were to become available. Such a development would provide an interesting test of the current objectives of the Society against a very different set of cultural values.

Surviving future crises

It also has to be accepted that the very rapid development of the Society over the past five years has almost certainly benefited from the fact that it has not to date

had to cope with any major crisis. Although it has faced serious problems as a result of poor security in the project area, these may in fact have contributed to its institutional development by necessitating a slow-down of field operations. A fast-moving crisis such as a renewed threat of famine, generalised insecurity such as existed in 1988, a major change of governmental policy (or even government), or an internal crisis would be a major test of the Society's institutional strength. Given Darfur's recent history, it is probable that the question is not *whether* but *when* the Society will have to undergo this test.

Replicability

One of the real tests of the project's effectiveness as a development trailblazer is likely to be its replicability. The Society itself has written the possibility of creating other similar organisations in other parts of Darfur or elsewhere in Sudan into its constitution. There are already moves towards some replication of the project's activities. The paravet initiative, built on the success of other Oxfam projects in south Sudan, has been used as the model for a similar scheme within the governmental structures in South Darfur by a former Kebkabiya Veterinary Officer.

As the demands made upon Oxfam's own operational capacity by the project have decreased, thought has been given to the possible replication or adaptation of the project in other parts of north Darfur. Staff who gained experience of working in the Kebkabiya project are have been retained within Oxfam's Darfur organisation. These staff are now at the forefront of investigating the possibility of replicating project activities in two other areas of North Darfur: the Dar-es-Salaam area close to El Fasher and the villages to the east of the Jebel Si mountain range directly adjacent to the current project area.

There has also been considerable interest in the project's success from within the governmental structure. Senior political figures have, on various occasions, cited it as a model of how an NGO can work to empower local people and it has even been featured on national television as such. Visitors from training and academic institutions and from other aid projects are a regular feature of the organisation's working calendar and there are at present discussions taking place with one of Sudan's leading tertiary educational institutions, Ahfad College for Women in Omdurman, for a group of students to visit each year to undertake study assignments.

The close working relationship with the Ministry of Agriculture which has for many years given the project official and technical support whenever needed has now started to feed benefits in the other direction. The Kebkabiya Agricultural Services Officer has been impressed by his contacts with Oxfam, working alongside El Hadi with the VEAs:

❛ Because of resource constraints I spent my first couple of months at Kebkabiya doing very little indeed and so I was really impressed by the sense of purpose when I first visited Oxfam and KSCS. I asked if I could accompany El Hadi on some of his field trips and discovered that he and the other staff really knew the community and the people's problems. I was also impressed with the way in which the different components work together to get a total picture of the development needs of a village rather than the different sectors working largely in isolation from each other.

Our problem at the Ministry office is finance and the help we've had from Oxfam has enabled us to make some impact. But more importantly, through the VEA system I've been able to pick up on an idea that could be used in our work. There are only two people working in agricultural services in the whole of Kebkabiya area, about three times the size of the KSCS project area! Even with better resources it would be quite impossible for us to do the job. However, using the VEA system would enable us to reach far more people and to make much more direct contact with the community. ❜

Handover as development

Perhaps the most important lesson is that handover is not a single action. To return to the analogy of the tent: Oxfam could not simply stop holding up the tent poles and walk away and expect the tent to remain standing. When it seemed that the handover would have to take place within a very short time-scale, there were real fears that the result might be a loss of everything that had been built up so carefully. When the apparent threat to Oxfam's presence had receded, the process of handover could proceed at a pace which has enabled relatively smooth progress. handover of the Kebkabiya project has involved a complex set of activities, which have been carried out in close consultation with the community. It has been, and continues to be, a step-by-step process that has taken time and patience, and that has been planned, implemented, and monitored like any other development activity. In that sense, the process of handover is simply a particular aspect of community development.

References

Adirondack, S and Macfarlane, R (1992) *Getting Ready for Contracts*, London: Directory of Social Change.

de Waal, A (1989) *Famine that Kills: Darfur, Sudan, 1984–5* Oxford: Oxford University Press.

Meadows, (1994) 'Kebkabiya Smallholders' Project Handover Evaluation', unpublished report, Oxfam.

Moser, C (1993) *Gender Planning and Development: Theory, Practice and Training*, Routledge.

Muir, A (1987) 'A reformulation of the Kebkabiya Smallholding Project, Darfur, Sudan', unpublished report, Oxfam.

Rodgers, B (1980) *The Domestication of Women*, Tavistock.

Strachan, P (1989) 'Kebkabiya Smallholders' Project: Phase Two Proposals', unpublished report, Oxfam.

Tout, K (1989) *Ageing in Developing Countries*, Oxford University Press.

Winch, A, Barrett, A and Ismail, M H (1992) 'Kebkabiya Smallholders' Project Evaluation', unpublished Oxfam report.

Glossary of Abbreviations

ITDG	Intermediate Technology Development Group
KSCS	Kebkabiya Smallholders Charitable Society
MSF	Medecins Sans Frontieres
NGO	Non-Governmental Organisation
PMC	Project Management Committee
SCF	Save the Children Fund
VCC	Village Centre Committee
VEA	Village Extension Agent

Oxfam Development Casebooks

other titles in the series include:

● **disabled children in a society at war**

A Casebook from Bosnia

Rachel Hastie

This Casebook analyses the lessons for working with disabled children learned from a radical and ambitious programme initiated by Oxfam UK and Ireland at the height of the war in Bosnia.

The book analyses issues such as working on long-term social development projects in an unstable society, and the impact of conflict on different groups of disabled people when disability itself becomes politicized.

0 85598 373 6

OXFAM
UK and Ireland

Oxfam (UK and Ireland) publishes a wide range of books, manuals, and resource materials for specialist, academic, and general readers.

For a free catalogue, please write to:
Oxfam Publishing,
274 Banbury Road,
Oxford OX2 7DZ, UK;
telephone (0)1865 313922
e-mail publish@oxfam.org.uk

Oxfam publications are available from the following agents:

for Canada and the USA: Humanities Press International, 165 First Avenue, Atlantic Highlands, New Jersey NJ 07716-1289, USA; tel. (908) 872 1441; fax (908) 872 0717

or southern Africa: David Philip Publishers, PO Box 23408, Claremont, Cape Town 7735, South Africa; tel. (021) 64 4136; fax (021) 64 3358.